Logan's Story

A Father's Fight Against The Fentanyl Crisis

Doug Ballinger Jr.

Doug Ballinger Jr.

ISBN : 979-8-89397-466-9

Edition: First

Published by Elite Scribes Book Writing

Doug Ballinger Jr.

57,834

That is the number of lives lost to fentanyl poisoning in 2020. Among them was my son, Logan. This is his story—his struggles, his triumphs, his battle with addiction, and the devastating reality of an epidemic that is stealing our loved ones too soon. But this book is not just about loss; it is about love, resilience, and the fight to break the stigma surrounding Substance Use Disorder. It is about the urgent need for better mental health support and real solutions to prevent more senseless deaths.

Through Logan's journey, I share my own transformation—from a grieving father to an activist, fighting for awareness, change, and justice for those still battling addiction. If you have ever felt helpless, if you have lost someone, or if you are searching for hope, know this: you are not alone. Together, we can turn pain into purpose and demand a world where compassion replaces judgment, and where no more families have to endure the heartbreak of losing a child to this crisis.

TABLE OF CONTENTS

Prologue: Breaking the Silence for Logan

The world was a little brighter whenever Logan walked into a room. It wasn't just his warm smile or his quick wit, it was the way he made everyone feel like they belonged. Logan had a gift for seeing the good in people, even when they couldn't see it in themselves. He was the guy who would pull over to help a stranger change a flat tire, the one who made sure the quiet kid at the party wasn't left out. He loved deeply, cared fiercely, and lived passionately. But Logan's story is more than the sum of his lighthearted moments and acts of kindness. It's a story of struggle, loss, and, ultimately, a call for change.

Logan was born on September 23, 1987, in Sarasota, Florida, to Doug and Gina, a couple whose love and hope for their son burned bright. From the start, Logan was a whirlwind of energy and curiosity, endlessly exploring and questioning the world around him. But as he grew older, life became more complicated. Diagnosed with ADHD as a child, Logan was introduced to the world of medication early. It was a double-edged sword, helping him focus but planting an insidious idea in his young mind: that there was a pill for every problem.

This belief, reinforced over time, became a silent undercurrent in Logan's life. Challenges that others might face head-on were instead numbed and buried under substances that promised relief. What began with prescribed medication evolved into something darker, as Logan turned to heroin to cope with

9

pain, guilt, and the pressure of life's expectations. Despite his addiction, his heart never wavered. He remained a champion of the underdog, a protector of the voiceless, and a beacon of joy for those lucky enough to know him.

Logan's journey with addiction was neither linear nor simple. There were moments of hope and times when he tried to fight back against the grip of heroin. He showed resilience, humor, and an unyielding desire to protect those he loved, even as he struggled to save himself. But addiction is a cruel thief, robbing its victims not only of their health and freedom but also of the relationships and moments that matter most. It steals quietly at first, then all at once.

In January 2020, Logan faced a devastating blow: the loss of his mother, Gina. She had been his anchor in many ways, a source of unconditional love even during his darkest moments. Her passing left a chasm in Logan's heart that no amount of support or love could fill. Just a few months later, on May 19, 2020, a week after Mother's Day, Logan's battle with addiction ended tragically. He died of fentanyl poisoning, a silent and deadly epidemic sweeping across the country.

This book is not just Logan's story; it's a story shared by countless families grappling with the devastating effects of addiction. It's about breaking the silence that surrounds substance use disorder and shining a light on the reality that addiction is not a moral failing but a disease. It's about raising awareness of the dangers of fentanyl, a drug so potent it's claiming lives at an alarming rate. Most importantly, it's about love, love for Logan, for those fighting addiction, and for the families left behind to piece their lives back together.

Logan's life was cut short, but his story doesn't have to end here. By telling it, we honor his legacy, his kindness, and his spirit. This is a father's journey through love, loss, and the hope that sharing his son's story will help save others. Logan's light may no longer shine in this world, but through these words, his legacy will continue to illuminate the path forward for others in darkness.

Chapter 1: A Bright Start

On September 23, 1987, the world welcomed Logan into its fold in the sunny city of Sarasota, Florida. Doug and Gina, his proud parents, were captivated the moment they laid eyes on him. He had a head full of hair and a pair of wide, curious eyes that seemed to take in everything around him. From the very beginning, Logan was a force to be reckoned with, a mix of boundless energy, unbridled curiosity, and an undeniable zest for life.

As a young boy, Logan was the embodiment of joy and chaos all rolled into one. He wasn't the kind of child to sit still for long. Whether he was racing around the house with a toy in hand or asking endless questions about how things worked, Logan's mind was always buzzing with activity. He was fascinated by the world around him, often stopping to admire animals, plants, or whatever else caught his eye. His love for creatures great and small was evident early on. Logan would go out of his way to rescue a stray cat or nurse an injured bird back to health.

Doug and Gina worked diligently to provide a stable and loving home for Logan. Gina had a nurturing presence, always ready with a hug or a word of encouragement. Doug, a steady and dependable figure, took pride in teaching Logan about responsibility and the value of standing up for others. Together, they made a great team, balancing each other's strengths to create a strong foundation for their son.

Logan's vibrant personality extended to the friends he made. From an early age, he had a magnetic quality that drew people to him. He was the kind of kid who could walk into a room of strangers and walk out with a dozen new friends. His laughter was infectious, and his generosity was boundless. Logan didn't just have friends; he had an ever-growing circle of people who adored and admired him.

But Logan wasn't just fun and games. He had a serious side too, one that reflected his deep sense of justice and compassion. He couldn't stand to see anyone being mistreated, whether it was a classmate being bullied or an animal in distress. Logan would leap into action, often putting himself in the line of fire to protect those who couldn't protect themselves.

Yet, behind the brightness, there were hints of the challenges to come. Logan's energy and curiosity sometimes felt uncontainable. School, with its structure and routines, was difficult for a boy who thrived on movement and discovery. His teachers often described him as intelligent but restless, full of potential but easily distracted.

Logan's story begins not only in Sarasota, Florida but in the quiet determination of two young parents trying to carve out a life of their own. When Logan was just eight months old, Gina and I decided it was time to leave Sarasota. Surrounded by the well-meaning but often overwhelming presence of her family, we felt it was important to step out on our own, to build a life with our son without the constant input of others, even when it came from a place of love.

Gina's parents, Grammy and Grandfather, lived in Sarasota, while my parents, Gran and Granddaddy, were in Memphis, Tennessee. Both sets of grandparents adored Logan and were eager to be a part of his life. But Gina and I felt the weight of their proximity and advice. We believed that, as young parents, we needed the space to figure out how to raise our child on our own terms.

Our new beginning took us to Arkansas, where we found refuge in a family lake house on Greers Ferry Lake. Nestled among the trees with the serene water as a backdrop, it became a temporary haven for our little family. There, Logan began to toddle around, his tiny footsteps echoing on the wooden deck. It was a simpler time in many ways, with no TV blaring or city noises to distract us. Instead, there was nature, quiet nights, and the laughter of an infant discovering the world.

Logan's first memories were likely shaped in that house. The lake, the trees, and the open space were his playground, and Gina and I soaked in the moments of watching our boy grow. He loved the water and would giggle uncontrollably when his tiny toes touched the cool lake. Even as a baby, Logan's boundless energy and curiosity were evident.

Eventually, it was time to move closer to opportunity. We made our way to Little Rock, where we found jobs and settled into an apartment. Life in Little Rock was challenging but full of promise. Like most young couples, Gina and I faced the usual struggles, balancing work and parenting, making ends meet, and learning how to navigate a marriage in the face of stress.

As Logan grew, so did the cracks in our relationship. Gina and I loved each other, but we began to see the world differently. Money was tight, emotions ran high, and small disagreements sometimes felt insurmountable. By the time Logan was two, Gina and I made the difficult decision to divorce.

Despite the separation, there was never a question about Logan's place in our lives. He lived with me, but Gina and I remained close friends, committed to raising our son together. We had an unspoken pact: no matter what happened between us, Logan would always come first. We worked hard to keep the coparenting relationship as seamless as possible. Gina was a constant presence in his life, and we maintained a level of respect and collaboration that many divorced couples struggle to achieve.

For Logan, this meant he grew up surrounded by love, even in a non-traditional family structure. He never doubted that both his parents were in his corner. Gina's warm and nurturing spirit balanced my steadiness and practicality. Together, we did everything we could to make Logan feel secure and loved.

As he moved into his toddler years, Logan's personality began to bloom. He was a ball of energy, running circles around adults with his endless curiosity and infectious laughter. He loved exploring, whether it was climbing on furniture or playing outside in the yard. Logan could turn any space into an adventure.

Even then, Logan's big heart was evident. He had a natural affinity for animals, always gravitating toward stray cats or dogs and begging to bring them home. It was as if he couldn't bear to see another living creature suffer. His love for the underdog, so central to who he became later in life, was already a core part of who he was.

The challenges of parenting a high-energy child like Logan were real, but Gina and I leaned on each other and found joy in the chaos. There were scraped knees, sleepless nights, and occasional tantrums, but there were also bedtime stories, spontaneous hugs, and the sound of Logan's laughter echoing through the house.

These early years laid the foundation for the person Logan would become, a boy full of life, love, and unyielding determination. They also set the stage for the challenges to come, as Logan's boundless energy and curiosity grew into something that didn't always fit neatly within society's expectations. But for now, Logan was simply a child discovering the world, and Gina and I were two parents doing our best to guide him through it.

When Logan was a little over three years old, life took another unexpected turn, one that added new depth and richness to our family dynamic. I met Scott, a kind-hearted and steady presence who would not only become my partner but also an integral part of Logan's life. Scott and I didn't wait long before introducing him to Logan, it just felt right. There was an instant connection between them, sparked by their mutual love for music and their easygoing spirits.

As Scott and I grew closer, he naturally stepped into the role of a parental figure for Logan. The three of us eventually moved in together, forming a new kind of family unit. While some might expect tension in such a situation, we were fortunate to have Gina's full support. Gina was as committed as ever to being present in Logan's life, and instead of seeing Scott as a competitor, she embraced him as part of the team. The three of us became an unlikely but effective parenting trio, bound together by our shared love for Logan and a common goal: to raise him with love, stability, and understanding.

Logan was the glue that held us all together. His boundless energy and infectious enthusiasm for life had a way of softening even the hardest of hearts. Scott and Logan developed a special bond, often over their shared love of music. Whether it was listening to records or singing along to tunes in the car, music became their shared language. Scott's patience and gentle nature made him a natural fit for Logan, whose spirited personality could sometimes be overwhelming.

Family events became a cornerstone of Logan's upbringing. Holidays, especially Thanksgiving and Christmas, were celebrated with gusto at our house. It was common to find our home filled with a lively and diverse group of family and friends. Gina was always invited and warmly included in every gathering. These celebrations were boisterous affairs, filled with laughter, good food, and a sense of love. Logan thrived in these moments, soaking in the joy and learning early on that family wasn't limited to blood relations, it was about the people who showed up for you, day after day, year after year.

Scott's mother, Miss Martha, also became an important figure in Logan's life. Their relationship was built on humor and affection, with constant teasing and playful banter. Miss Martha had a knack for bringing out Logan's silly side, and he adored her for it. She, in turn, doted on him, treating him as one of her own.

Traveling to visit family became another cherished tradition. On holidays, we would often make the trip to Memphis to see my parents, Gran and Granddaddy. These visits were a mix of warm Southern hospitality and the kind of comfort that only grandparents can provide. Logan was showered with love and attention, whether it was through Granddaddy's stories or Gran's home-cooked meals.

Gina and Logan also made trips to Florida to visit her parents, Grammy and Grandfather. These visits were just as meaningful, giving Logan a chance to build memories with his maternal side of the family. Despite physical distance, there was never a lack of love or connection. Logan quickly learned that family wasn't bound by geography, it was in the effort to stay close, to be present for one another, even across the miles.

Logan's childhood was full of love, laughter, and the understanding that family could take many forms. He grew up surrounded by people who adored him and who worked together, despite their differences, to ensure he felt secure and cherished. Gina's unwavering presence, Scott's steady influence, Miss Martha's humor, and the love of his grandparents on both sides gave Logan a strong foundation. He learned early on that family meant more than shared DNA, it was about shared experiences, mutual support, and unconditional love.

This unorthodox but deeply loving family dynamic helped shape Logan into the person he was. It showed him that relationships could thrive in unexpected ways and that people could come together, not out of obligation, but out of love and commitment.

As Logan grew older, he carried these lessons with him, though life's challenges sometimes made it difficult for him to hold on to the sense of stability and love that had defined his early years. But even as he faced those challenges, the seeds of love and connection planted in his childhood remained a part of him, guiding his actions and shaping the way he cared for others.

From an early age, Logan developed a deep love for Lebanese food, a love that was about more than just the flavors. For Logan, the food was a gateway to understanding his heritage, a window into the lives of the ancestors who had come before him. Gran's family was 100% Lebanese, and through her, I had inherited the rich culinary traditions of our lineage. Growing up, I learned to cook the traditional dishes from my grandmothers and great-grandmothers on my mother's side of the family. These weren't just cooking lessons; they were family history lessons, woven with stories of immigration, love, and resilience.

When I passed these traditions down to Logan, it was like inviting him into a centuries-old conversation. He watched intently as I prepared kibbeh, grape leaves, tabbouleh, and baklava, asking questions about each step of the process. His curiosity wasn't limited to the food itself, he wanted to know the stories behind it. He would sit at the kitchen counter, his wide eyes fixed on me, and ask, "Who first made this? Did they bring it from Lebanon? What's the special meaning of this dish?"

Logan's inquisitiveness made cooking with him a joy. He saw every ingredient and every recipe as a key to unlocking the past. When I shared the stories I had learned from my grandmothers, his face lit up. He was especially fascinated by the tales of how our ancestors immigrated to America, braving unknowns to build a life for their families. He loved hearing about how they met, fell in love, and got married, often against the odds, and how they worked tirelessly to provide for their children.

The stories brought the food to life for Logan. He didn't just see a table laden with Lebanese dishes; he saw the people who had made it possible for us to sit together as a family and share a meal. He understood that every grape leaf rolled, every pan of kibbeh baked, was an act of love and a link in the chain of generations that led to him.

Southern comfort food also had a special place in Logan's heart. I learned to cook these traditional dishes thanks to my Mamaw, my father's mother. My dad's mother had passed down her knowledge of hearty, soul-soothing dishes that were staples of our Southern upbringing. From fried chicken and biscuits to collard greens and chocolate pie, these meals were another layer of family tradition that Logan eagerly soaked in. Logan saw no division between the Lebanese and Southern influences in our family, they were simply different threads of the same tapestry.

For Logan, food wasn't just sustenance. It was storytelling, connection, and love. He recognized that a big family feast was never just about eating, it was about coming together, sharing lives, and honoring the people who had come before us. He would sit at the table, his plate piled high with a mix of grape leaves and turkey and listen intently as the grown-ups reminisced about the past. He loved hearing about Gran and Granddaddy's adventures, Grammy and Grandfather's lives in Florida, and how Scott's family traditions blended into the mix.

These moments in the kitchen and at the dinner table were more than just family rituals, they were lessons in identity and belonging. Logan learned that his family wasn't just the people sitting beside him; it was the generations of hardworking, resilient individuals who had come before. They were in the food, the stories, and the love that surrounded him every day.

This sense of connection and tradition stayed with Logan throughout his life. Even as he faced challenges and struggled with his own demons, the lessons he learned from those early years, about love, resilience, and the importance of family, remained a core part of who he was.

Chapter 2: Early Challenges

Being a young parent is like setting off on a journey without a map. You're faced with decisions that feel monumental, and you have no way of knowing how they'll shape the road ahead. For Gina, Scott, and me, raising Logan was a team effort, but like most parents, we often found ourselves navigating unfamiliar terrain. Logan was a bright, inquisitive, and energetic child, but as he transitioned into school, some challenges began to emerge.

Logan had difficulty concentrating in the structured environment of the classroom. His boundless energy, which made him such a joy at home, often clashed with the rigid expectations of school. Teachers described him as intelligent but easily distracted, capable but unfocused. The school's recommendation was clear: Logan should be evaluated by a professional.

We wanted to do right by our child, so we took him to a doctor associated with Children's Hospital. At the time, this seemed like the logical next step. We were told Logan had attention deficit hyperactivity disorder (ADHD), a term that was unfamiliar to us but explained many of the behaviors his teachers had described. The doctor assured us that there was a solution, a pill that could help Logan focus, behave "appropriately," and succeed in school.

The recommendation to start Logan on Ritalin came quickly, with little room for discussion. We were told this was the best course of action, and as young parents without any experience to draw from, we trusted the experts. The doctor's authority, combined with the school's support of the diagnosis, left us feeling like this was the answer we had been searching for.

Gina, Scott, and I discussed it extensively. Like any parents, we wanted the best for Logan, and the promise of a solution that could "fix" his behavior and help him thrive in school was hard to ignore. After weighing the options, we agreed to start Logan on the medication.

Looking back, with the clarity of hindsight, we can see how this decision, made with the best intentions, was the start of a subtle but significant shift in Logan's life. The introduction of Ritalin sent an unspoken message: taking a pill could make everything better. It wasn't something we realized at the time, but this lesson would echo throughout Logan's life in ways we couldn't predict.

The use of Ritalin (methylphenidate) to treat ADHD in children has been widely studied, and it can offer significant benefits while also posing potential drawbacks.

Ritalin is intended to Improve focus and attention. It is a stimulant that increases the availability of dopamine and norepinephrine in the brain, enhancing the ability to focus, sustain attention, and control impulsive behaviors. Many children with ADHD experience noticeable improvements in academic and social settings. Studies show that Ritalin can reduce hyperactivity and impulsivity, leading to better interactions with peers, teachers, and family members. While not a cure for ADHD, Ritalin often allows children to better complete schoolwork and engage in learning by managing their symptoms.

Common side effects included loss of appetite, insomnia, stomach aches, headaches and increased heart rate and blood pressure. These can lead to difficulty maintaining a healthy diet or sleeping patterns.

Some children report feeling "flat" or less expressive while on the medication. Others experience mood swings, irritability, or heightened anxiety as the medication wears off. Ritalin is a stimulant and has a potential for misuse or dependency, particularly in adolescents and young adults. Logan complained of feeling wiped out at the end of the day but we continued the medication.

Critics argue that ADHD medications like Ritalin sometimes perpetuate a "quick fix" mentality, potentially overshadowing non-pharmaceutical interventions such as behavioral therapy, counseling, or lifestyle changes. Although there was counselling for Logan and our family to help manage his behavior, at the time it did not seem to be centered on his "mental wellness" and had little to do with helping him with what he was feeling. The focus seemed to be more on managing his behavior with meds and discipline.

Being on medication for ADHD can sometimes lead to stigma, affecting the child's self-esteem and how they are perceived by others.

Ritalin can be a highly effective treatment for managing ADHD in children, significantly improving their quality of life and ability to function in structured environments. However, it is not without its challenges, and careful consideration must be given to potential side effects, misuse, and the importance of a comprehensive treatment plan.

At first, the results were promising. Logan was able to focus better in school, and his teachers noted improvements in his behavior. For a while, it seemed like the Ritalin was working, and we felt relief. But the deeper implications of that choice, on Logan's understanding of how to cope with challenges, were far less visible.

Logan was still the same amazing child we were all working to raise. He was curious, loving, and fiercely protective of those around him. But as we later came to understand, the medication didn't address the root of his struggles. It quieted the symptoms but didn't teach Logan the skills to navigate his emotions, impulses, or challenges. In a way, it masked deeper issues instead of helping him learn how to face them.

The stigma surrounding behavioral challenges also played a role in our decision. Society often labels children who don't fit neatly into the mold of a traditional classroom as "difficult" or "problematic." As parents, we wanted to shield Logan from those labels. The idea that a medication could make him "normal" was enticing, not because we wanted to change who he was, but because we wanted to protect him from a world that wasn't always kind to children who were different.

We couldn't have known then that this early experience would plant a seed in Logan's mind: the belief that pills could solve problems. At the time, all we saw was our bright, energetic son who had been handed a challenge, and we did what we thought was best to help him overcome it.

As parents, we face impossible choices, often with incomplete information. Looking back, it's easy to see how this path shaped Logan's understanding of himself and the world.

But in those moments, all we wanted was to give him the tools to succeed, to show him he was loved and supported, and to create an environment where he could thrive.

Logan remained the remarkable, big-hearted child we all knew and loved. He adapted quickly, finding his own rhythm even as the world tried to fit him into its structures. But the subtle lessons from those early years, the reliance on medication, the unspoken message that his natural energy needed to be "fixed", would quietly linger.

This chapter of Logan's life is a reminder of how parenting, even with the best intentions, is an act of trial and error. We were doing the best we could with the information we had, guided by love but not always by clarity. And through it all, Logan continued to teach us as much as we were trying to teach him, about resilience, curiosity, and the power of love to navigate even the toughest challenges.

Medication became a constant presence in Logan's life. While it helped him focus, it also marked the beginning of a pattern. Logan began to view it as a solution to his problems, an easy way to fix things rather than facing the consequences of his actions. This mindset wasn't entirely his fault, it was the narrative that society often placed on children with diagnoses like his.

Despite these challenges, Logan's heart remained as big as ever. He continued to advocate for the underdog, becoming a protector of anyone who needed help. Whether it was a friend struggling with their own challenges or an animal in need, Logan was there. His empathy was boundless, and he seemed to instinctively know when someone was hurting.

But underneath the surface, cracks were beginning to form. Logan's struggles with ADHD, combined with the pressure to succeed in a traditional academic environment, began to take a toll on his self-esteem. He started to internalize the idea that he was different, that he didn't quite fit the mold.

Chapter 3: A Childhood Interrupted

Logan was about eight years old when I got the phone call every parent dreads. There had been an accident on the playground, and Logan had gotten injured. My heart sank as I listened to the voice on the other end, describing the situation in careful but urgent tones. They couldn't tell me much over the phone, only that Logan had fallen and was in the school office. I hung up and immediately called Gina and Scott. Within minutes, we were all racing to the school, converging there almost simultaneously.

When we arrived, we learned that Logan had been playing a game of chicken with Tanner, one of his school friends. The challenge?

Balancing on a landscape timber in the playground. It was classic Logan, always ready for a bit of fun and competition, completely in the moment, not thinking about the "what ifs." This time, though, the "what ifs" became reality. Logan had lost his balance, spinning around and falling off the timber. He landed awkwardly, his leg catching against the timber as he fell. The result was a spiral fracture in his femur, the largest bone in his body.

By the time we arrived, Logan had already been taken to the school office, where he was being cared for as best as possible. Seeing him there, pale and in pain but trying to put on a brave face, was both heart-wrenching and reassuring. He was scared but still cracking small jokes, trying to ease the tension for everyone else in the room, a glimpse of his enduring spirit even in tough times.

It was clear he needed medical attention immediately, so the school arranged for an ambulance to transport him to the hospital. Gina, Scott, and I followed closely behind, our minds racing with worry and questions. I tried to stay calm for Logan's sake, but the moment I saw the X-rays, my composure cracked. The spiral fracture in his femur looked terrifying, a vivid reminder of how fragile and vulnerable our children truly are. For a few moments, I couldn't hold back the tears. My son was hurt, and there was nothing I could do to take away his pain.

The doctors explained that Logan would need surgery right away. They would apply an external fixator, a medical device to stabilize his broken femur while it healed. The fixator would look like something out of a science fiction movie, with metal rods extending out from his leg to keep the bone in place. It was a lot to process, but the priority was clear: Logan needed to heal.

The surgery went smoothly, and Logan was incredibly brave throughout the ordeal. When we saw him post-surgery, there he was, our eight-year-old boy, with a complex medical device sticking out of his leg and a tiny walker by his bedside. Despite everything, he still managed a smile. Logan's resilience shone through even in the face of pain and discomfort.

For the first few days, we were all on high alert, hovering around Logan to make sure he was comfortable and cared for. But it quickly became clear that Logan had no intention of letting this injury slow him down. He adapted to the walker with surprising ease, navigating the house with determination. If the fixator was a burden, he never let it show. His sense of humor remained intact, and he often joked about the contraption sticking out of his leg. He refused to let it define him.

To give Logan the best possible start to his recovery, we decided to send him to Memphis to stay with Gran for a while. There's nothing quite like the care of a grandmother, and Gran poured all her love and attention into helping Logan heal. She made sure he ate well, kept him entertained, and encouraged him every step of the way. Under her watchful eye, Logan's recovery began in earnest.

Logan's time in Memphis became a special chapter of his recovery journey. Gran had a knack for making the tough days feel manageable and even fun. Logan thrived under her care, learning to maneuver his walker like a pro and figuring out how to navigate life with the external fixator. He approached it like a challenge rather than a setback, showing maturity and strength beyond his years.

After three months, the fixator was finally removed. Logan was thrilled to regain his freedom, but the experience left behind some lasting reminders: four small scars, two on his hip and two above his knee. Always one to find humor in the little things, Logan affectionately referred to the scars as "cat butts," a nickname that stuck and became part of the family's inside jokes.

Looking back, I don't recall if pain medication played a significant role in Logan's recovery. At the time, it seemed like the focus was more on managing his discomfort through rest and care than relying heavily on medications. If painkillers were used, they weren't as prominent or as readily prescribed as they would become in later years.

This incident was a formative experience for Logan, and for all of us. It tested his resilience, his adaptability, and his ability to find humor even in difficult circumstances. It also reinforced just how strong he was, both physically and emotionally. For us as parents, it was a stark reminder of how unpredictable life can be and how deeply we want to protect our children, even when we can't shield them from every fall.

Through it all, Logan showed us that even in the face of pain, he could find a way to keep moving forward, literally and figuratively. This was just one chapter in his life, but it was a testament to his determination and the love that surrounded him as he healed.

Chapter 4: A New Chapter in Florida

When Logan was around ten years old, life presented us with another big opportunity, and challenge. I was offered a chance to move to Fort Lauderdale, Florida, to open a multilingual service center. It was an incredible step forward in my career, but it also meant uprooting our lives in Little Rock. The decision wasn't one I could make lightly. I discussed it extensively with Scott, his family, Gina, and my parents. Together, we weighed the pros and cons, knowing that any change would ripple through Logan's life as well.

Ultimately, we decided this was an opportunity worth taking. I would move to Fort Lauderdale almost immediately to begin the work, while Scott stayed behind to pack up our house and prepare it for sale. My mom and I traveled to Florida together to look for a new home, a task that proved both exciting and overwhelming. After some searching, we found what felt like the perfect house in a community called Margate.

The Margate house was more than just a home, it felt like a fresh start. Set on a beautiful freshwater canal, it offered a tranquil view that instantly made us feel at ease. The backyard was a dream, complete with a screened-in lanai and a sparkling swimming pool. I could already picture Logan splashing around in the water, laughing and playing as he always did. It felt like a place where we could thrive as a family.

I knew that Logan needed more than just a great house, he needed his mother. One of the first things I did when I accepted the position was to negotiate a role for Gina in the Fort Lauderdale office. It was important to me that she be nearby, not just for Logan but for the continuity of our parenting team. Gina found an apartment just two blocks away from the new house. The canal separated our homes, but if it hadn't been for the water, it would have been a minute-and-a-half walk between us. This proximity made it easy to maintain the close co-parenting relationship we had worked so hard to build.

For Gina and me, moving back to Florida felt like a return to familiar ground. It was a chance to reconnect with the state where Logan was born and where so many of our early memories as parents were made. For Scott, however, this was uncharted territory. He had lived his entire life in Arkansas, and moving to Florida marked a significant change. He approached it with a sense of adventure, eager to embrace the new surroundings and opportunities that came with the move.

The transition was a whirlwind. Logan, always adaptable, took the news in stride. He was curious about what life in Florida would be like and excited by the idea of living near a pool and canal. He was particularly drawn to the promise of warm weather year-round, perfect for his high-energy personality and love of outdoor activities.

Once the move was complete, the new arrangement quickly fell into place. Logan could easily move between our homes, spending time with both Gina and me while maintaining the stability of his routine. The close-knit dynamic we had built in

Little Rock transferred seamlessly to Florida, with Scott now part of the team as we navigated this new chapter together.

Living in Margate brought a sense of renewal for all of us. The house became a hub of activity, filled with Logan's laughter and the hum of daily life. Logan loved the pool, spending countless afternoons diving in and perfecting his cannonballs. The canal added a sense of serenity, a backdrop to family dinners on the lanai and lazy weekends spent soaking up the Florida sunshine.

Gina's apartment became an extension of our shared life. Logan would often dart back and forth between our homes, treating both spaces as his own. The arrangement allowed us to maintain a sense of cohesion in our parenting, ensuring that Logan always felt supported and surrounded by love.

For Scott, the move was an opportunity to broaden his horizons. He embraced life in Florida with enthusiasm, taking in the new sights and experiences that came with living in a vibrant and diverse community. His steady presence continued to be a grounding force for Logan, and their bond grew even stronger as they shared this new chapter together.

Through it all, Logan's resilience and adaptability shone. He was curious about his new surroundings and eager to explore and make friends. Florida became a backdrop for his boundless energy and growing personality, a place where he could thrive in the warmth of both the sun and the love that surrounded him.

This move marked a significant milestone in our family's journey. It wasn't just about relocating, it was about building a life that reflected our values, our love for one another, and our commitment to providing Logan with the best possible foundation. Florida gave us a fresh start, a chance to continue shaping our story together.

Chapter 5: A Home Full of Life

Settling into life in Florida didn't just mean a new house, new jobs, and new routines, it also meant opening our doors to family and friends from across the country. It seemed as if the sunny warmth of Florida, combined with the love that radiated from our home, made it impossible for anyone to stay away for too long.

Visitors came in waves, especially during the colder months. My mother, ever the energetic and determined matriarch, was a frequent guest. She would often stay for a week at a time, and every visit brought her signature touch, rearranging the furniture. I can't count the number of times we'd walk into a room during one of her visits and find the couch in a new spot or the chairs swapped out. It became a running joke in the family, and Logan would sometimes try to predict which room she'd transform next.

Miss Martha, Scott's mother, also became a cherished seasonal fixture. She had a standing tradition of arriving shortly after Christmas and staying until around Easter. Her presence brought warmth and steadiness to the household. She and Logan continued their playful banter, and she became a beloved part of the fabric of our family life.

One year, my mother decided that Scott and I would host Thanksgiving at our house in Florida. This wasn't just a small family dinner, it was a full-blown gathering of relatives, friends, and loved ones. Gina was, of course, part of the festivities, as were friends and a long list of family members. My brother JD brought his daughters, Elizabeth and Callie, down to join us, and even my father's dad, Papaw, made the trip. The house was buzzing with excitement, filled to the brim with people, love, and laughter.

Thanksgiving dinner was a beautiful blend of traditions. Alongside the classic turkey and trimmings, we served traditional Lebanese dishes, connecting our present to the rich history of our ancestors. The table was piled high with tabbouleh, kibbeh, and grape leaves, sitting comfortably next to a turkey, stuffing, mashed potatoes, and cranberry sauce. It was a feast in every sense of the word, a celebration of diversity and love that defined our family.

Logan, as always, was in his element. He thrived in the lively atmosphere, moving easily from guest to guest, and sharing jokes and stories. He loved having Papaw there, soaking up the stories and wisdom of his great-grandfather. Watching Logan engage with family during moments like this always filled me with pride. He had such a way of making everyone feel special, bridging generational gaps with his charm and warmth.

After the meal, when the dishes were cleared and the excitement began to wind down, the family settled in for a movie. Scott took a picture that captured the essence of the day: my father, my brother JD, my mother, Elizabeth, Logan, Callie, and me all piled onto the sectional sofa, ready for a quiet moment together after the day's festivities. It was a snapshot of a perfect moment, one that spoke to the unshakable bond of our family and the joy of being together.

The distance between Florida and the rest of the family was never an obstacle. If anything, it gave everyone an excuse to visit, to escape the colder climates up north, and to gather in a home that felt like a refuge. Our house in Florida wasn't just a place where we lived; it was a gathering spot, a hub of love and connection that drew people in and made them feel welcome.

Logan learned so much from these gatherings. He saw firsthand the value of family, of maintaining connections even across distances. He understood that love and belonging weren't bound by geography, that they lived in the effort people made to show up for one another. These experiences helped shape his deep sense of loyalty and his ability to bring people together, traits that would remain central to who he was throughout his life.

Even years later, when I think back to that Thanksgiving or the countless other gatherings we hosted, I feel an overwhelming sense of gratitude. Those moments weren't just about food or tradition, they were about the bonds we shared, the laughter that filled the air, and the love that seemed to spill out of every corner of our home. And at the center of it all was Logan, soaking it in, contributing to it, and being shaped by it.

Chapter 6: Preteen Years

Life in Florida seemed to suit Logan. He quickly made friends in the neighborhood, his outgoing nature making it easy for him to connect with others. It was a joy to see him flourish in the sunny, laid-back environment of our new community. Logan had a knack for finding common ground with people, and his ability to make others feel special was evident even at a young age.

Scott would sometimes bring Logan to my office to visit me. Those visits were a highlight of my day. Logan was always respectful, his natural charm winning over everyone in the office. He had a way of putting people at ease, cracking jokes, and making even a professional environment feel a little brighter. Having him and Scott visit added a touch of normalcy to our otherwise unconventional lives, a reminder that no matter how busy or chaotic things became, the family was at the center of everything.

But as Logan entered his preteen and early teenage years, things began to shift. Like many kids his age, he started testing boundaries and pushing our patience. He became more defiant at times, less willing to follow rules, and more prone to emotional outbursts. Scott, Gina, and I often found ourselves wondering: Was this normal teenage behavior? Was it a side effect of his ADHD? Or were we missing something deeper?

It's a question that haunted me. I didn't want to jump to conclusions, but I also didn't want to dismiss the changes in Logan's behavior. He wasn't turning into a "bad child," and I knew that deep down. Logan was still the loving, compassionate, and curious boy we had raised. But he was also struggling in ways we didn't fully understand.

In hindsight, I realize we likely should have sought professional guidance. Logan's struggles weren't unique, many kids with ADHD and other behavioral challenges benefit from counseling or therapy to help them navigate their emotions and impulses. At the time, though, it didn't feel urgent. Logan wasn't in crisis; he wasn't failing out of school or getting into serious trouble. His behavior seemed like typical teenage rebellion, something that would pass with time.

What we didn't realize was that these years were critical. Logan was learning how to cope with frustration, disappointment, and the pressures of growing up. Without the tools to manage his emotions in a healthy way, he began to lean on the lessons he had learned earlier in life, the idea that external fixes, like medication, could "solve" his problems. Unintentionally, we had left a door open for addiction to take hold later.

It's hard to look back on these years without feeling a pang of regret. We were doing our best, navigating the complexities of parenting with love and good intentions. But we didn't fully understand what Logan needed, and in our effort to keep things moving forward, we missed the opportunity to delve deeper into his mental health.

Counseling could have helped Logan understand himself better. It might have given him tools to manage his ADHD, process his emotions, and build resilience. It might have given us, as parents, the insight we needed to support him more effectively. But those realizations only came later, when it became clear how deeply Logan was struggling.

Still, there were plenty of bright moments during those years. Logan's charm and humor remained intact, and he continued to shine in social settings. His ability to make people laugh and feel at ease was unmatched, and he carried that skill into his friendships and interactions with adults. He loved making others happy, a trait that endeared him to everyone who knew him.

Looking back, I see those years as a mix of joy and missed opportunities. Logan was growing up, testing limits, and figuring out who he was. He wasn't a "bad kid" or a "problem child." He was simply a boy navigating a world that didn't always make sense to him, trying to find his place. And while we may have missed some chances to help him along the way, the love we shared as a family was always there, providing a foundation that kept us connected through the challenges ahead.

Chapter 7: The Teenage Years

As Logan grew into his teenage years, the challenges became more pronounced. His energy, charm, and desire to connect with others, qualities that had always been his strengths, now seemed to lead him into situations where he was searching for acceptance, even at a cost. At school, Logan started getting into more trouble. Small issues escalated, and his behavior began raising flags with teachers and administrators. He wasn't failing academically, but his focus and motivation seemed to waver. Outside of school, Logan was finding himself drawn to a crowd that didn't always have his best interests at heart.

It's hard to pinpoint when things began to shift. At first, everything seemed normal. Logan started attending sleepovers and making friends in the neighborhood. From the outside, it looked like he was just being a typical teenager, spending time with peers, figuring out his identity, and pushing boundaries as kids often do. But then came a weekend that raised questions I didn't fully have the answers to.

Logan returned home after staying the weekend at a friend's house. When he walked through the door, I immediately noticed his hair, it had been twisted into small dread knots. It was a stark departure from his usual style and seemed out of character. I couldn't help but feel a wave of concern, though I couldn't yet articulate why.

"The first thing you need to do," I told him, "is get in the shower, wash your hair, put conditioner in it, and brush it out until it's gone."

Logan didn't like hearing that. For him, the hairstyle was probably a symbol of fitting in, trying on a new identity, and being accepted by the group he was spending time with. For me, it felt like a red flag, a sign that he was trying too hard to fit into a crowd that might not have his best interests at heart.

We went back and forth for a while, but eventually, Logan honored my request. He washed out the knots and brushed his hair back into its usual style. I didn't push further at the time, but a nagging feeling lingered. Looking back, I suspect this was one of the first times Logan had experimented with drugs. Whether it was marijuana, alcohol, or something else, I couldn't say for certain. However, the shift in his demeanor and behavior suggested that something was beginning to change.

At the time, it was hard to find the balance between giving Logan the freedom to grow and protecting him from the risks that seemed to surround him. We didn't want him to feel trapped, like a prisoner in his own life. We thought that giving him a bit more freedom, a chance to make his own decisions, might help him settle down and find his way. But in hindsight, we see that this approach may have backfired.

Living in Southeast Florida added another layer of complexity. It was a vibrant, fast-paced place, full of opportunities but also full of temptations. Drugs and alcohol weren't hard to come by, and for a teenager like Logan, curious, eager to fit in, and not always mindful of the long-term consequences, these things were all too available.

Logan was still the amazing, big-hearted boy we'd always known. He was full of life, always quick with a joke or a smile, and deeply caring toward others. But we couldn't ignore the changes that were happening. His mood seemed to shift more often. His focus was scattered. And while we couldn't put our finger on exactly what was happening, we sensed that Logan was wrestling with something bigger than just typical teenage rebellion.

It's easy, in hindsight, to see the signs we missed. At the time, it felt like we were doing everything we could, giving him love, guidance, and space to grow. But addiction doesn't announce itself loudly at first. It creeps in quietly, disguised as experimentation or rebellion. We missed the signs that Logan was beginning to take steps down a path that would lead to deeper struggles.

As parents, we wanted to believe that Logan's strong sense of right and wrong, his natural charm, and his resilience would steer him back on course. But adolescence is a complicated time, and Logan's desire to fit in, combined with the pressures of growing up and managing his ADHD, left him vulnerable in ways we didn't fully understand. On several occasions Logan expressed his desire to stop taking the Ritalin because it made him feel "blah" and he didn't think it was helping him.

That weekend, with the twisted dreads and the battle over washing them out, became a small but telling moment. It was a glimpse into the internal conflict Logan was navigating, the pull between wanting to find his place in the world and the difficulty of staying true to himself. It's a moment I wish I'd delved deeper into, not to judge or reprimand, but to understand what he was feeling and why.

The environment in Southeast Florida, so full of possibility but also full of risk, became a backdrop for Logan's teenage years. He was a boy on the cusp of adulthood, trying to find his footing in a world that wasn't always kind or forgiving. And though we didn't know it at the time, those years would be the start of a journey that would test him, and us, in ways we couldn't yet imagine.

Chapter 8: Summers in Memphis

Summers in Memphis were always a highlight for Logan. He loved the chance to visit Gran and Granddaddy, escaping the routines of home in Florida and diving into a world of adventure, creativity, and bonding with his grandparents. These trips weren't just vacations, they were opportunities for Logan to connect deeply with two of the most influential people in his life, forming memories and lessons that would stay with him forever.

Granddaddy was Logan's partner in exploration. Together, they spent hours tinkering in the garage, fixing up cars, and tackling projects that required more ingenuity than precision. Granddaddy loved sharing his knowledge with Logan, who soaked it all in, eager to learn and be a part of whatever his grandfather was working on. Whether it was a rusty car part that needed fixing or a shiny motorcycle ready for a ride, Logan was at Granddaddy's side, ready to get his hands dirty.

Motorcycle rides were a special treat. Logan's face would light up when Granddaddy would fire up the bike, the growl of the engine signaling a new adventure. They'd ride through the backroads of Memphis, the wind whipping through their hair and the world speeding by. Those rides were more than just fun, they were a chance for Logan to feel free, a way for him to bond with Granddaddy in a way that words couldn't capture.

The mini-storage buildings and the pawn shop were another source of excitement. Granddaddy would take Logan along to work, showing him the ins and outs of running a business. Logan loved the hustle and bustle of the pawn shop, the stories behind the items people brought in, and the negotiations that played out. It was a world of people and treasures, and Logan thrived in the mix of curiosity and connection.

Gran, on the other hand, was Logan's guide to style and sophistication. They would spend hours shopping, scouring every store in Memphis for the newest fashions and the best deals. Logan loved it, not just the clothes but the time spent with Gran. She had a knack for finding bargains, and Logan would proudly show off the treasures they found together when he returned to Florida. New shoes, trendy outfits, and accessories that made him feel confident and cool, it all came from those long shopping trips with Gran.

At the lake house, Logan was in his element. The peaceful retreat provided endless opportunities for adventure and connection. Fishing trips with Granddaddy were a favorite, where patience and excitement blended perfectly as they cast their lines into the water. The lake wasn't just a place to fish; it was a space to relax, bond, and enjoy the beauty of nature. Logan would also ride four-wheelers with Gran and Granddaddy, zipping through trails and feeling the thrill of the ride.

Logan was about six or seven years old when Granddaddy and Uncle Walt decided it would be a great idea to gift him a tiny, gas-powered four-wheeler. It was an exciting moment for Logan, his first taste of independence on wheels. Everyone gathered in the driveway of the lake house to watch him learn how to ride. Logan was beaming with excitement, ready to tackle this new adventure.

At first, everything was going well. Logan was cautiously navigating the four-wheeler, his little hands gripping the handlebars tightly as he listened to instructions from Granddaddy and Uncle Walt. He quickly got the hang of it, his confidence growing with every pass in the driveway. The whole family was cheering him on, proud of how brave and determined he was.

Then, in a flash, everything changed. Logan suddenly veered off course, bolting down the hill on the side of the house. The four-wheeler sped out of control, heading straight toward a tree. Being so young, Logan didn't fully understand how to stop. Driven by fear, he kept his tiny hand clamped down on the throttle, which only made the situation worse.

Before anyone could react, Logan lodged himself between the four-wheeler and the tree. The driving wheel spun against the back of his calf, causing a minor injury. At that moment, I felt my heart drop. Instinct kicked in, and without hesitation, I sprinted down the hill to rescue my son.

When I reached him, Logan was terrified, clutching the handlebars with a grip fueled by fear. I quickly snatched him out from between the four-wheeler and the tree, pulling him into my arms. His arms immediately wrapped around my neck, and he began screaming directly into my ear. The sound was deafening, but I knew it was pure fear driving his reaction.

I ran back up the hill with Logan clinging to me like a lifeline. My mother, always the calm and practical one in a crisis, met us at the house and directed us straight to the shower. She turned on the cool water and began running it over Logan's injured leg to soothe the burn caused by the spinning wheel. Logan was still screaming, the shock and fear of the incident overwhelming him. To keep him from screaming directly into my ear, we handed him a washcloth to bite down on. It was a small but effective solution that gave everyone's ears a much-needed break.

As the cool water ran over his leg and the adrenaline began to wear off, Logan finally started to calm down. The injury turned out to be minor, nothing more than what a little antibiotic ointment and a bandage couldn't fix. The whole family let out a collective sigh of relief, grateful that it hadn't been worse.

Within a short time, Logan was back to his usual self, laughing and running around the lake house as if nothing had happened. But we all knew we needed to be a bit more cautious with the four-wheeler moving forward. Granddaddy and Uncle Walt made sure to supervise him even more closely, and we established stricter rules for when and where he could ride.

This incident, while frightening at the moment, became one of those family stories that we told again and again, often with laughter. It was a testament to Logan's resilience, how he could face a scary situation, recover quickly, and jump right back into the swing of things. It was also a moment that underscored the deep bond between Logan and his family. In his time of need, he had all of us rallying around him, ready to protect and care for him.

Looking back, the four-wheeler incident was more than just a scary memory. It was a snapshot of Logan's adventurous spirit and the love and dedication of the people around him. Logan didn't let fear define him, even as a child. He learned to face challenges head-on and move past them, traits that would remain a central part of who he was throughout his life.

One of the most memorable gifts Granddaddy gave Logan was a PT Cruiser, a few years before Logan was even old enough to drive. The car became a project for them to work on together during Logan's visits. They would spend hours adding aftermarket bling, turning the Cruiser into something uniquely Logan. It was a labor of love and a bonding experience that deepened their relationship. For Logan, the PT Cruiser wasn't just a car, it was a symbol of the care and attention Granddaddy poured into their time together.

When Logan returned home to Florida, he was always excited to share the stories of his adventures and show off the new clothes and shoes Gran had helped him pick out. His pride was palpable, not just in the material things but in the experiences and the love that had gone into every moment of his time in Memphis.

Those summers weren't just about fun, they were about connection, discovery, and the special bond Logan shared with Gran and Granddaddy. The lessons he learned, the skills he picked up, and the memories he created became an integral part of who he was. Memphis wasn't just a place; it was a sanctuary, a second home where Logan could be himself, surrounded by love and the steady presence of two people who adored him.

As Logan moved further into his teenage years, parenting him became increasingly challenging. His growing independence clashed with our efforts to guide him, and his attitude began to reflect a warped sense of entitlement and a desire to live without the restrictions of being parented. For Gina, Scott, and me, it felt like we were running out of options to help him find his footing.

Logan wasn't inherently defiant or malicious; he was navigating the complex emotions and pressures of adolescence in a way that often pushed against the boundaries we tried to set. His charisma and intelligence sometimes masked his struggles, making it difficult to pinpoint how to best support him. Somewhere during this turbulent time, my brother JD stepped in with an offer that seemed like a potential solution.

JD suggested that Logan come live with him in Memphis. The move offered Logan a fresh start, a chance to step out of his current environment and find a new rhythm to his life. In Memphis, he'd be surrounded by family, particularly his cousins Elizabeth and Callie, and he'd have an opportunity to work at JD's gas stations. We all hoped that this change would provide Logan with stability, responsibility, and a sense of purpose.

When Logan moved to Memphis, it didn't take long for JD to introduce him to the gas station business. Logan quickly picked up the skills necessary to work in the stations, from customer service to stocking shelves and managing day-to-day tasks. JD also began teaching him about cars and mechanic work, a passion that had been sparked during his summers spent tinkering with Granddaddy. Logan's natural aptitude for mechanics became apparent almost immediately. He had a sharp eye for detail and a problem-solving mindset that made him adept at diagnosing and fixing issues.

Logan approached the work with enthusiasm, often diving in headfirst and sometimes overanalyzing every situation. While his tendency to overthink could occasionally slow him down, it also demonstrated his commitment to doing things right. He didn't want to cut corners; he wanted to understand the full picture and ensure the job was done properly.

His time in Memphis wasn't just about work, it was about reconnecting with family. Living with JD allowed Logan to form a closer bond with his uncle, who became both a mentor and a guide. His cousins Elizabeth and Callie added another layer of connection and support, giving Logan a sense of belonging that was different from what he had experienced at home. The change in environment gave him a chance to step into a new role, one where he could learn, grow, and prove himself.

Logan thrived in certain aspects of his life in Memphis. His work ethic shone through in the gas stations and on the mechanic jobs he took on. He found pride in his accomplishments, and it was clear that when Logan put his mind to something, he could excel. He was meticulous and creative, often finding innovative ways to approach problems.

However, even in this new setting, Logan's struggles didn't completely disappear. The freedom he gained by moving away from home came with its own set of challenges. While JD provided structure and guidance, Logan was still a teenager trying to balance his desire for independence with the responsibilities placed on him. The habits and influences that had begun to take root in Florida didn't vanish overnight, and Logan continued to wrestle with the complexities of adolescence and self-discovery.

During his time in Memphis, Logan gave us a glimpse of what he was capable of when he found something that captured his interest. His ability to apply himself to his work, his natural curiosity, and his determination to succeed were evident in everything he did. Logan's time with JD reminded us that he wasn't defined by his challenges; he had the capacity to grow, learn, and thrive when given the right opportunities.

Still, the road ahead was uncertain. While the move to Memphis brought moments of stability and success, it wasn't a cure-all for the deeper struggles Logan faced. It was a step, a chapter in his life that highlighted both his potential and the ongoing challenges of navigating a world that didn't always make sense to him.

Chapter 9: A Move Back to Arkansas

Life has a way of bringing us full circle. Not long after Logan moved to Memphis to live with JD, another series of changes began to unfold. Gina decided to change jobs and move back to Sarasota to be closer to her family, her parents and brothers. Around the same time, my job in Florida came to an end. With Logan in Memphis, Gina in Sarasota, and our chapter in South Florida coming to a close, Scott and I made the decision to move back to Arkansas.

It was a bittersweet moment. Florida had given us so many wonderful memories, from family gatherings to sunny days by the pool, but it was time to let it go. We put a plan in place to list the house in Margate for sale and prepare for our next move. The house sold quickly, and with the money we made, we were able to purchase a beautiful house in Fairfield Bay, Arkansas.

Fairfield Bay wasn't just a move; it was a dream realized. Nestled on Greers Ferry Lake, the mountain-top home we bought was nothing short of breathtaking. The view stretched out for miles, a serene and tranquil backdrop that felt worlds away from the fast pace of Florida. It was the perfect place to begin our next chapter, offering peace, beauty, and a sense of grounding that we hadn't realized we needed.

Scott's family was thrilled to have us back in Arkansas, close enough for frequent visits. After years of living in Florida, it felt good to be near them again, reconnecting and re-establishing those bonds. Scott's mother, Miss Martha, had always cherished her winter visits to South Florida, but even she found joy in coming to Fairfield Bay for extended stays. The beauty of the area, combined with the comfort of being near family, made it a natural adjustment for everyone.

Life in Fairfield Bay moved at a slower, more deliberate pace. Gone were the constant visits from friends and family escaping the northern winters and the bustling energy of South Florida. In their place was a quiet rhythm, punctuated by the sound of the wind through the trees and the lapping of the lake against the shore. It was a welcome change, one that allowed Scott and me to breathe, to reflect, and to appreciate the simplicity of our new surroundings.

Miss Martha became a frequent guest, her visits filled with warmth, laughter, and the steady presence she always brought to our lives. Her humor and wisdom were constants, and she loved spending time with us in Fairfield Bay, surrounded by the beauty of the mountains and the lake.

While Fairfield Bay offered tranquility, it also offered connection. Scott's family was nearby, and the visits from his siblings and extended family reminded us of the deep roots we had in Arkansas. The sense of belonging we felt in Fairfield Bay wasn't just tied to the house or the view, it was tied to the people who surrounded us, and the relationships that enriched our lives.

By this time, Logan was still in Memphis, growing into his independence and finding his way. The physical distance between us wasn't easy, but we remained connected, always keeping a line of communication open. Logan would call to update us on his life, sharing stories of his work at the gas stations, his time spent with his cousins, and his latest projects with Granddaddy.

Though we were separated by miles, Fairfield Bay became a place where Logan could visit, a home he could always return to when he needed to recharge or reconnect. The house on the mountain-top, much like the lake house he had loved as a child, offered a sense of sanctuary, a place where he could escape the pressures of the world and feel grounded in the love of his family.

Once we settled into our home at Fairfield Bay, life began to take on a new rhythm. The peaceful surroundings of this small community were a welcome change, and it wasn't long before decisions were made that would bring even more family together. Logan decided to leave Memphis and come live with us, finishing out his high school years in Arkansas. It felt like another fresh start, with our family closer and new memories waiting to be made.

As the holidays approached, my mother, ever the planner, decided Scott and I would host Christmas again, this time in our Fairfield Bay home. JD and his girls, along with my mom and dad, stayed at the lake house on the other side of the lake. Meanwhile, we were at home, busy transforming our space into a magical holiday retreat.

Our one-acre lot, covered with towering trees, became a canvas for Christmas lights. Every tree shimmered with twinkling bulbs, turning the yard into a radiant forest. The house itself glowed with festive cheer, adorned with lights that sparkled like stars. Inside, we went all out, decorating with 15 full-sized Christmas trees. Each room held its own unique tree, some themed and others bursting with a riot of colorful ornaments. The house was transformed into a winter wonderland, a magical escape that brought joy to everyone who visited.

Across the street lived Lera and Sandra, a duo who quickly became dear friends. Lera, remarkably, was just over 100 years old, and Sandra, in her mid-60s, served as her devoted companion and caregiver. There was an instant connection, and soon we were spending more and more time with them. They invited us to join them at church, and through this bond, we became more active in Peace Lutheran Church.

The church community welcomed us with open arms. Pastor Sue, a compassionate and wise woman, became a cornerstone of support in our lives. Her warmth and guidance were invaluable, and she had a knack for making people feel seen and heard. In the years that followed, Pastor Sue's kindness would become a lifeline, offering comfort and counsel during difficult times.

Lera and Sandra were especially enchanted by our Christmas display. Lera, despite her advanced age, had a childlike wonder for the holidays. She would sit by her front window for hours, gazing at our brightly lit forest across the street. The sight of the trees glowing against the dark winter sky seemed to bring her immense joy.

Our home and yard became a beacon of light, not just for our family but for the entire neighborhood. It was a reminder of the magic that could be created with a little effort and a lot of love, a testament to the power of community, celebration, and the bonds we form with those around us.

With the house transformed into a haven of Christmas cheer and our traditional multicultural feast prepared, the anticipation for Christmas Eve celebrations was palpable. Every corner of our home sparkled, and the aroma of spices and festive treats filled the air, a symphony of sensory delight.

Early in the afternoon, my family arrived. True to form, my mother wasted no time inspecting the house. She moved from room to room, ensuring every decoration was just so, and nothing was out of place. Her discerning eye for detail was legendary in our family. The kitchen was her next stop, where she observed my preparations with her usual blend of love and critique. Cooking and decorating during the holidays were a long-standing, friendly rivalry between us, each of us vying to outdo the other in creating the most magical holiday experience.

Despite the lighthearted competition, the shared goal of crafting a perfect Christmas brought us closer. Logan was especially thrilled to have everyone gathered at our house this year. He darted between conversations, grinning ear to ear, soaking in the joy of having family close for this special holiday.

As the afternoon faded into evening, the lights on our property began to glow. The timer ticked, and suddenly the entire yard was alight, the trees shimmering with color. Just as the first lights flickered on, nature added its own touch of magic, it began to snow.

The snow fell gently at first, a soft dusting that quickly turned the landscape into a scene straight out of a Norman Rockwell painting. The glowing lights were enhanced by the falling snow, their colors refracting through the frosty air. Inside, the woodburning stove crackled, adding warmth and comfort to the bustling house. Family and friends milled about, chatting, snacking, and enjoying the feast that had been lovingly prepared.

The food was a reflection of our family's diverse tastes, a mix of traditional holiday dishes and multicultural favorites that had become staples of our celebrations. Plates were piled high, and laughter filled the air, blending with the soft strains of Christmas music in the background.

As the evening progressed, the snow began to accumulate, forming a pristine, glittering blanket across the yard. By the time it reached about an inch, my parents decided it was time to head back to the lake house with Papaw, JD, and the girls. It was dry snow, the kind that crunched softly underfoot, and though the roads remained passable, my mother, ever cautious, insisted they make the trip before conditions worsened.

We stood on the porch, watching as they made their way to their car, the snowflakes swirling around them. The soft glow of the Christmas lights illuminated the scene, turning it into a postcard-perfect moment. As they drove off, their taillights disappearing into the snowy night, we felt a sense of gratitude for the time spent together, the warmth of family, and the magic of a holiday well celebrated.

The holiday season had barely passed when life threw me an unexpected curveball. Scott, who had been visiting family in Little Rock and helping a friend prepare for a sidewalk sale, was supposed to return home on Sunday evening. As the time for his arrival approached, I received a phone call from him, a call that would change everything.

At first, I thought it was a simple delay. He said he wasn't coming home, and in my naivety, I assumed he meant he'd be staying in Little Rock for a few extra days. But then he clarified, and the words hit me like a punch to the gut: he wasn't coming home, ever.

As the shock settled in, the reality of the situation became clear. This wasn't a spur-of-the-moment decision. Over the past couple of weekends, Scott had been quietly taking his clothes and belongings to Little Rock, preparing to start a new chapter without me. It was a decision he'd made while I was blissfully unaware, carrying on with our daily lives.

The news left me reeling. My mind raced with questions and emotions, anger, sadness, confusion, and a deep sense of loss. How had I missed the signs? What could I have done differently?

In the days and weeks that followed, I began to confront some hard truths. Relationships, I realized, require effort and understanding from both sides, and ours had not been without its challenges. I wasn't always the easiest person to live with. I could be stubborn, quick-tempered, and, at times, downright difficult. I had moments where I was less kind than I should have been, less patient than I needed to be, and less present than I wanted to be.

Scott's departure forced me to look inward, to examine the ways I had contributed to the cracks in our relationship. It was a painful process, but it also became a turning point.

Though Scott's leaving was a devastating event in my life, it turned out to be a moment of profound growth. The pain didn't disappear overnight, but in time, I came to understand that his choice wasn't just about my flaws or his desires, it was about two people who had grown apart and needed different things.

Life went on, as it always does. The house that had been a winter wonderland just weeks before now felt quiet and empty. Looking back, I can see that while Scott's departure was a heartbreak, it also set me on a path I wouldn't have found otherwise, a path toward self-awareness, resilience, and eventually, peace.

Amid the emotional whirlwind following Scott's sudden departure, a bright spot emerged, a reminder that even in the darkest times, there are moments of grace. One of Logan's closest friends, Daniel, came to stay with us, and his presence turned out to be one of the best things to happen during that difficult period.

Daniel was the kind of young man who left an impression. Raised in the country, he had a gentle, kind soul that belied his upbringing in a place where many kids struggled to escape cycles of hardship. But Daniel was determined to carve a different path for himself. His ambition and inner strength were remarkable for someone his age. While he occasionally showed a streak of wildness, like any teenager, he was maturing into a truly exceptional young man.

Chapter 10: A Brotherly Bond

Logan and Daniel were practically inseparable during this time. They spent hours together, talking, laughing, and finding ways to make the days feel lighter. They shared a brotherly bond that went beyond simple friendship. For Logan, Daniel's companionship was a lifeline, providing support and distraction during a time when everything seemed uncertain.

But Daniel's presence wasn't just a comfort to Logan, it was a blessing for me, too. Both boys did everything they could to console me after Scott left, often offering words of encouragement or simply their quiet company when I needed it most. Daniel had an uncanny ability to sense when I was struggling and would offer his unassuming support without any need for recognition or thanks.

Over time, Daniel became more than just Logan's friend, he became family. I began to think of him as a bonus child, someone who had been woven into the fabric of our lives through love and shared experiences. Watching him grow and navigate the challenges of young adulthood was a privilege, and I found myself cheering him on as if he were my own.

Even now, years later, I remain in contact with Daniel. The bond we formed during that tumultuous period has only grown stronger with time. He holds a special place in my heart, and I am proud to call him part of my extended family.

Chapter 11: Finding Strength in the Struggle

After Scott left, I realized that I needed to make changes in my life, not just to cope with the heartbreak but to find a new sense of purpose and control. One of the biggest changes I decided to focus on was my weight. It was a battle I had faced my entire life, fighting against both my genetics and my love for good food. This time, I was determined to win. So, I took a step that would change everything: I joined the gym at Fairfield Bay.

For a small, country town, the gym at Fairfield Bay was surprisingly well-equipped. It had an indoor pool, primarily used for water aerobics, an indoor basketball court, a complete set of weight training machines, and even an indoor track. It felt like a hidden gem, a place that had everything I needed to start this new chapter.

When I first visited the gym to sign up, they mentioned an upcoming promotion that would waive the joining fee if I waited a week. But I knew myself well enough to recognize that if I didn't join that day, I likely wouldn't come back, not because of them, but because I needed to act on my determination while it was fresh. I told them as much and signed up right then and there. That decision marked the beginning of a journey that would redefine my life.

The trainers at the gym were incredible. They helped me ease into my new routine, teaching me how to stretch properly and setting up a circuit of weight machines combined with walking on the indoor track. At first, I was skeptical about walking the track, dismissing it as unnecessary since I was focused on losing weight. Little did I know that cardio would become the cornerstone of my transformation.

The next day, armed with my headphones and an iPod filled with the saddest country songs I could download from Napster, I started working out. It wasn't easy. There were days when I cried uncontrollably while walking the track or pushing through the weight machines, mourning the life I thought I'd lost. But I kept going. The gym became my sanctuary, a place where I could pour all my emotions into something productive.

At first, the changes were subtle. My body began to respond to the exercise, and the weight started to come off. Encouraged by the progress, I pushed myself further. What started as a tentative stroll around the track grew into a routine of walking 40 laps a day. Each lap was a testament to my resilience, each mile a symbol of my determination to take back control of my life.

The gym community was another source of strength. Everyone was kind and supportive, cheering me on and understanding the emotional and physical struggles I was facing. They didn't just see me as someone trying to lose weight, they saw me as someone fighting to rebuild themselves.

Over the course of 10 months, I shed 180 pounds, going from a weight that had once defined and confined me to a leaner, healthier version of myself. By the end, I was down to 225 pounds, a weight I hadn't seen in years. The transformation wasn't just physical; it was emotional, mental, and spiritual. I had unlocked something inside me, a sense of discipline and perseverance that had always been there but had been waiting for the right moment to shine.

This journey was more than a weight loss story. It was a story of reclaiming my identity, proving to myself that I could face hardship and come out stronger. The gym became a place where I found not only strength in my body but also strength in my spirit, a place where I discovered the power of pushing through pain to reach something better on the other side.

In the aftermath of heartbreak and the intense journey of rebuilding my physical health, I recognized that my mental well-being also needed attention. The house on the mountain, with its beautiful views and countless memories, had become a reminder of a life I was ready to move on from. The time had come to let it go and start fresh.

After some searching, I found the perfect place to start over, a charming three-bedroom, two-bath condominium nestled on a golf course overlooking a serene lake. The condo featured a cozy, all-weather enclosure in the back that felt like an oasis of peace, a place where I could unwind and reflect without being overwhelmed by the past.

The new space was exactly what Logan, Daniel, and I needed, a blank slate. Moving into the condo marked the beginning of a new chapter, one focused on creating fresh memories and finding joy in the present.

It didn't take long for Logan and Daniel's friends to discover our new home. The condo quickly became a central hangout spot, buzzing with the energy of teenagers coming and going. The boys filled the space with laughter, video games, and endless conversations about the things that mattered to them, school, friendships, and dreams for the future.

I didn't mind the constant activity. In fact, I welcomed it. The lively atmosphere made the condo feel like a home, and it brought me comfort to know that Logan and Daniel had a supportive group of friends who cared for one another. Watching them all interact gave me hope and reminded me of the power of community in healing.

The condo offered more than just a change in scenery; it provided a much-needed shift in perspective. From the tranquil views of the lake to the sense of freedom from the weight of old memories, the new home became a sanctuary. It was a place where I could breathe, process, and begin to truly move forward.

The laughter and camaraderie of the boys filled the condo with life, turning it into a space of connection and joy rather than isolation and sorrow. It was a reminder that healing isn't always about being alone to reflect, sometimes it's about surrounding yourself with energy, love, and the promise of things to come.

Deciding to sell the house at Fairfield Bay was not an easy choice, but it was necessary. The house held too many memories of a life I was ready to move beyond. Once the decision was made, I called Scott to let him know of my plans. I explained that Logan, Daniel, and I would be moving into a condo and that I intended to use the proceeds from the house sale to purchase new furniture, creating a fresh start in our new place.

I had no interest in holding onto most of the furniture from the Fairfield Bay house. It seemed fitting to part ways with it as I moved forward. I proposed a deal to Scott: if he and his brother would come up to Fairfield Bay to help us move a few essential items and our personal belongings to the condo, we would assist him in loading the remaining furniture onto a truck for him to take back to Little Rock for his new house.

Scott agreed to the arrangement. It felt like a fair compromise, one that allowed us to part ways without conflict or unnecessary emotional strain.

When moving day arrived, it was a surprisingly smooth process. Scott and his brother came as promised, and we worked together to sort through the house. I took only what I truly needed and wanted, items that held meaning to me or served a functional purpose in the new condo. The rest of the furniture was packed onto Scott's rental moving truck for him to take to his new home.

The process, though bittersweet, was civil. There were no arguments, no lingering animosity, just a shared understanding that this was a necessary step for both of us to move forward with our lives.

As the truck pulled away with the last of the furniture, I stood on the porch of the house at Fairfield Bay one final time. There was a sense of closure at that moment. I wasn't just leaving behind a house, I was leaving behind a chapter of my life that had shaped me in ways I was only beginning to understand.

The peacefulness of the move set the tone for the fresh start I was embarking on. It wasn't about erasing the past but about creating a future where I could focus on growth, healing, and the people who mattered most to me.

Chapter 12: A New Path for Logan

Even after settling into our new life at the condo, challenges remained, particularly for Logan. At Shirley High School, a small, close-knit school in our rural community, he was struggling to concentrate and stay focused on his work. It was frustrating for both of us to watch his potential overshadowed by these difficulties, but I knew that with the right environment, he could thrive.

One of the blessings of this small country school was the dedication of its teachers and administrators. They genuinely cared about their students, going above and beyond to ensure each child had the chance to succeed. They saw Logan's potential and recognized that traditional classroom settings might not be the best fit for him. Instead of letting him fall through the cracks, they presented us with an alternative.

The school offered Logan the opportunity to join a self-paced study program, allowing him to complete his coursework on his own schedule while still meeting all the requirements to graduate on time. It was a flexible and supportive solution, one that gave him the chance to take control of his education.

We jumped at the opportunity. The self-paced program turned out to be exactly what Logan needed. Freed from the pressures of a traditional classroom, he began to excel. The ability to move at his own speed and focus on his strengths allowed him to rediscover his confidence and sense of purpose.

I watched with pride as Logan flourished. He tackled his studies with newfound determination, and his success in the program proved what I had always known, he was capable of great things when given the right tools and environment.

I will always be grateful to the administrators and teachers at Shirley High School for seeing Logan as an individual and giving him this chance to succeed. Their willingness to think outside the box made all the difference in his life, turning what could have been a challenging situation into an opportunity for growth.

Logan's success in the program became a beacon of hope for both of us. It reminded me that with the right support, we can overcome obstacles and find new ways to thrive, even when the path isn't clear at first.

One of the aides at the Shirley Alternative Learning Center (SALC), Miss Angie, saw Logan not as a challenge but as a person who just needed a little extra attention. In a letter I later found among Logan's belongings, she addressed the stigma he faced and emphasized the importance of recognizing that every human is unique. I am deeply grateful to Miss Angie and the entire SALC team at Shirley High School. They saw my son as an individual with value and potential, not as someone to be discarded simply because he didn't fit a predetermined mold. Their kindness and understanding made all the difference at that time and Logan was able to graduate with his class.

Chapter 13: A Lesson on Responsibility

Life with teenagers is never dull, and Logan's high school years were no exception. When he moved to Fairfield Bay, he wasn't driving the PT Cruiser because it had been in an accident. Instead, he had a sporty little red car that he was quite proud of. That car became part of a story that none of us would soon forget, a story that tested not only Logan's maturity but also my patience and resolve as a parent.

It started one morning while I was at the gym, feeling strong and fabulous in my workout clothes, my muscles pumped and my spirits high. That's when my phone rang. On the other end was someone from Logan's school, telling me that I needed to come in immediately. They assured me Logan was safe but mentioned that he had done something requiring my immediate attention. Without hesitation, I left the gym and headed straight to the school.

By the time I arrived, I had pieced together the story. Logan and Daniel had been on their way to school, stopping to pick up a couple of friends along the way. Logan was driving, and apparently, they had passed a car on a double yellow line. That alone would have been bad enough, but Logan had been trying to light a glass weed pipe while steering the car with his knees. To make matters worse, the passenger had taken over steering duties during this stunt.

As if the scenario weren't absurd enough, the car they passed belonged to none other than the principal of Shirley High School. You'd think the boys might have recognized the car, but no. The principal, understandably shocked, immediately called the school to report what had just happened.

When Logan and his entourage arrived at the school parking lot, they were met with flashing lights, a police officer and school administrators waiting for them.

I pulled into the parking lot, still in my string tank top and workout clothes, my headphones hanging around my neck. The scene felt surreal, part comedy, part nightmare. The officer and administrators briefed me on the situation and told me they needed my permission to search the car since Logan was a minor.

Without hesitation, I granted it.

The search turned up nothing but the glass weed pipe. No marijuana, no additional paraphernalia, just the pipe. Logan, to his credit, immediately took responsibility, admitting that it was his pipe and ensuring his friends wouldn't face consequences for his actions.

After hearing Logan's admission, the officer decided to let him off with a stern warning. Since no drugs were present and Logan had owned up to his mistake, the situation didn't escalate into anything more serious. The school, however, imposed a three-day in-school suspension, a punishment that seemed both fair and manageable.

While I was furious and embarrassed at the moment, I also couldn't help but feel a strange sense of pride in Logan for stepping up and taking responsibility. It was an early test of his character, and though his actions had been reckless and immature, his willingness to own up to them was a glimmer of hope that he was learning the value of accountability.

That day at the school was a turning point, a reminder that parenting teenagers is as much about guiding them through their mistakes as it is about celebrating their victories. And Logan, for all his antics, was a teenager worth believing in.

Chapter 14: Adventures on the Boat

During this part of our lives, the pontoon boat became our floating sanctuary. It wasn't anything fancy, just a previous rental boat I had purchased from the marina, but it was perfect for us. The boat gave Logan, Daniel, and me an escape from the world, a place where we could be ourselves, talk openly, and create unforgettable memories.

Many afternoons were spent out on the water, gliding across the lake, listening to music, and soaking in the sun. The boat became a haven for laughter and life lessons. Conversations ranged from silly to serious as we floated aimlessly, letting the gentle waves guide us. Music was always part of the experience, our soundtrack to these moments was eclectic and full of soul, from rock classics to reflective ballads.

I had a habit of embarrassing the boys, something I took great delight in. One of my favorite antics was wearing a Speedo, which left Logan mortified every single time. Daniel, however, found the entire thing hilarious, both because I was wearing a Speedo and because Logan was so comically distressed about it. The contrast between their reactions made it even more entertaining for me.

Occasionally, my love for the unconventional would take us on nocturnal adventures. In the middle of the night, I'd wake Logan and Daniel and announce, "Let's go out on the boat." At first, they'd grumble, half-asleep, but soon they'd get caught up in the excitement of doing something so out of the ordinary.

We'd pile into the car, drive to the marina under the cover of darkness, and quietly climb aboard the boat. Slowly, we'd make our way to the middle of the lake, the hum of the motor fading as we cut the engine and drifted into the stillness of the night.

Out there, surrounded by the pitch blackness of the water and the sky, the world seemed to pause. We'd lie back, gazing up at a spectacular display of stars, the Milky Way arching above us in a dazzling show of cosmic wonder. I'd play music fitting for the moment, Moody Blues, Pink Floyd's Dark Side of the Moon, or something equally transcendent, and we'd float, lost in the enormity of the universe.

We never stayed out too long, just enough to feel the profound awe of our surroundings and to connect in a way that only happens in the stillness of the night. These midnight trips were spontaneous and unconventional, but they were deeply meaningful. They embodied everything I wanted for Logan and Daniel: an appreciation for the beauty around them, a sense of wonder, and the freedom to embrace life's unplanned moments.

The time we spent on that pontoon boat remains some of the most precious moments of my life. It wasn't just about the boat or the lake; it was about being together, finding joy in simplicity, and forging bonds that would last a lifetime. Those nights under the stars, the laughter, and even Logan's exaggerated embarrassment over my Speedo are memories I hold close to my heart.

In many ways, the boat symbolized our journey, drifting through uncertain waters, guided by love, laughter, and the belief that even in the darkest times, there's beauty to be found.

Chapter 15: Quilts of Love and Blessings

As the days grew longer and the air warmer, it became clear that Logan and Daniel were approaching a major milestone: high school graduation. It was a time filled with anticipation, reflection, and preparation for the next chapter of their lives. At the same time, my involvement in Peace Lutheran Church brought a beautiful tradition into our lives that would mark this moment with love and care.

Peace Lutheran Church was more than just a place of worship for me, it was a community that embraced me during a pivotal time in my life. One of the most touching traditions of this church was its annual celebration for soon-to-be graduates. On the Sunday before high school graduation, the congregation honored the graduating seniors in a unique and heartfelt way.

The members of the church created handmade quilts, each one a labor of love. These quilts were carefully folded and draped over the pews, turning the sanctuary into a vibrant display of colors and patterns. During the service, Pastor Sue offered a special blessing, surrounding the quilts, and the young people who would receive them, with prayers for guidance, protection, and comfort as they embarked on their next journeys in life.

One of the few times Logan and Daniel joined me at church was for this special occasion. On that day, the sanctuary was filled with an atmosphere of warmth and celebration. The sight of the quilts draped over the pews was striking, a tangible representation of the love and support of our church community.

During the service, Pastor Sue spoke about the challenges and opportunities that lay ahead for the graduates, encouraging them to carry with them the lessons they had learned and the faith that would guide them. When it was time for the presentation, Logan and Daniel each received a quilt made by the hands of people who cared deeply for their future.

The gesture was more than just symbolic; it was a physical reminder that they were surrounded by love and support, no matter where life took them. Logan, ever reserved in moments like this, quietly accepted his quilt, while Daniel wore a smile, appreciating both the gift and the occasion.

The quilts from Peace Lutheran Church were more than just practical items, they were symbols of connection, faith, and community. In the years to come, I hoped Logan and Daniel would look at their quilts and remember that they were never alone and that they carried with them the love of a congregation that believed in their potential.

For me, it was a bittersweet moment. Watching Logan and Daniel receive their quilts marked the end of one chapter and the beginning of another. It was a reminder of how far we had come as a family and how much more lay ahead.

As they stood there, holding their quilts and surrounded by a congregation that had embraced us, I felt a deep sense of gratitude, for the church, for Pastor Sue, and for the journey that had brought us to this moment.

Chapter 16: Senior Prom

High school senior prom is a rite of passage, a night that marks the end of high school and the start of the rest of their lives. For Logan and Daniel, it was no different. The excitement of this milestone grew as the date approached, and the boys began plotting how to make their prom night memorable. One of their ideas, of course, involved my Cadillac.

Logan and Daniel came to me with a proposal: they wanted to borrow my Cadillac to pick up their dates and arrive at prom in style. At first, I hesitated. Logan's track record when it came to responsibility wasn't exactly spotless, and the thought of entrusting my car to a couple of teenagers on one of the most high-energy nights of their lives made me nervous.

Still, after much deliberation, and no small amount of parental angst, I decided to give them the chance. This was their moment, after all, and I didn't want to be the roadblock to what could be a cherished memory. With my blessing came a stern reminder about safety, responsibility, and the privilege of using the Cadillac.

Once the car situation was settled, we turned our attention to the other essentials of prom night. Picking out their outfits became a mission, with the goal of finding something that would not only make them look sharp but also complement their dates' dresses. The boys took it seriously, trying on suits and ties, debating colors and styles, and ultimately settling on ensembles that struck the perfect balance of sophistication and personality.

The day of the prom was filled with anticipation. Logan and Daniel spent hours primping and perfecting their looks. They had detailed the Cadillac earlier in the week, ensuring it was spotless and ready for its big moment. When the time came, they posed for pictures, looking every bit the part of confident young men stepping into their futures.

As they drove off, I was left to wrestle with my nerves. While I wanted to trust Logan, the "what-ifs" lingered. My parental instincts battled with my determination to give him the space to create his own memories.

To occupy my mind, I turned to the distractions of the early internet. MySpace had just emerged as the hot new platform, and while connecting with people online wasn't as seamless as it is today, it offered a place to lose myself for a while. I spent the evening chatting, downloading music from Napster, and praying everything would go smoothly.

When the boys finally walked through the door at the end of the night, looking tired but happy, a wave of relief washed over me. They were safe, the car was in one piece, and the night had been everything they'd hoped for. For once, everything had gone as planned, and they returned with stories of laughter, dancing, and the magic of prom.

For me, it was a lesson in trust and letting go, realizing that sometimes, we have to step back and give our children the chance to prove themselves. Logan and Daniel had risen to the occasion, and their prom night became a memory we could all cherish.

Chapter 17: Graduation Day

Graduation day was fast approaching, and with it came the opportunity to gather the people who had shaped Logan's life and supported him along the way. It was a milestone not just for Logan and Daniel but for all of us who had played a part in raising them. To celebrate, we sent out invitations to everyone who mattered, family, friends, and loved ones, and, to my delight (and slight apprehension), nearly everyone RSVP'd with an enthusiastic "yes."

The guest list was a mix of personalities and histories: Gina, her parents Grammy and Grandfather; my parents Gran and Granddaddy; JD and his girls; and, yes, Scott and his family. Everyone made plans to come, and they were arriving with bells on. My family stayed at the lake house about 30 minutes from Fairfield Bay, while we arranged for two additional condos in the Time Share rental units, one for Gina and her parents and another for Scott and his family.

The reunion was an exercise in diplomacy, but it was also a testament to how far we had come as co-parents and extended family. It had been a long time since Gina, Scott, and I had all been in the same place at the same time. While the thought made me a little anxious, I was determined to focus on the celebration and the incredible achievement of seeing Logan graduate.

To kick off the festivities, my mom hosted a dinner at the Fairfield Bay Country Club for everyone who had traveled from out of town. It was a wonderful gesture, bringing together people who had supported Logan and Daniel through the years. Even

Daniel's mother joined us, though her health challenges kept her from fully participating in the celebration.

As I walked into the dinner, I couldn't help but feel a little self-satisfied. Here I was, surrounded by my son's mother, my ex, and their families, but I was physically fit, confident, and, if I do say so myself, looking fantastic. It was a reminder that the best revenge is good living, and I was living well.

The evening turned out to be a surprisingly pleasant affair. The shared pride in Logan and Daniel helped dissolve any lingering tensions, and the focus remained squarely on the boys and their accomplishments. We laughed, shared stories, and enjoyed a delicious meal in celebration of two young men who had worked hard to reach this milestone.

The next day was the big event. Everyone dressed to the nines, Logan and Daniel in their caps and gowns, looking both nervous and excited, while the rest of us donned our best attire to mark the occasion. The entire entourage made its way to Shirley High School for the ceremony.

As the boys walked across the stage to receive their diplomas, I was overwhelmed with pride. Seeing Logan in that moment felt like a culmination of years of effort, love, and resilience. The challenges we had faced together, the moves, the struggles, the moments of doubt, all led to this day. And it was worth every single bit of it.

I wasn't just proud of Logan for graduating; I was proud of all of us, his parents, his family, and the community that had supported him. This was a shared victory, a testament to what could be accomplished when people put aside differences and come together for the sake of their children.

After the ceremony, we gathered for pictures, hugs, and more laughter. Logan and Daniel beamed with pride, their accomplishments shining through their grins. We celebrated as a family, and for that day, it didn't matter who was related to whom or what history might have existed between us. It was a day for unity, love, and honoring the bright futures ahead of these two boys.

This milestone marked not just the end of Logan and Daniel's high school journeys but the beginning of their next adventures. And for me, it was a moment to reflect on how far we had all come, and how much promise lay ahead.

Chapter 18: New Connections

After the whirlwind of Logan's graduation and the dust from the celebrations settled, life returned to a quieter rhythm. But in the stillness, a new chapter was quietly unfolding. For nearly a year, I had been chatting with someone online, a person who, over time, had become an unexpected source of connection, understanding, and intrigue.

Randy and I met in one of those early internet chat rooms, back when the online world felt like a vast and exciting frontier. As our conversations grew more personal and engaging, we moved away from the chaotic chatter of public rooms to the more intimate space of Yahoo Messenger. It became a daily ritual, logging on, sharing thoughts, and exploring the depths of our ideas about the world.

We talked about everything: relationships, dreams, our views on life, and the intricacies of the human experience. There was an ease to our conversations, a sense that we could speak freely without judgment. It wasn't just small talk; it was the kind of dialogue that made you think, reflect, and laugh all at once.

Over time, our virtual connection deepened. We shared occasional pictures, giving each other glimpses into the lives we led behind the screens. Randy had a warmth and wisdom about him that drew me in. Though our conversations existed entirely online, they were real in every sense of the word. The distance between Fairfield Bay and Memphis felt insignificant compared to the closeness we had built through words.

Each day, I looked forward to our chats, wondering what new topics we might delve into or what stories he might share. Randy became a bright spot in my life, a connection that seemed to hold the promise of something more.

As our conversations continued, the thought of meeting in person began to surface. It wasn't an idea I approached lightly, there was always a risk in translating an online connection into real life. But with Randy, it felt like a natural progression. The more we talked, the more I felt that this was someone I wanted to meet, someone who could potentially become a part of my life beyond the glow of a computer screen.

Memphis wasn't far, just a few hours' drive, and the idea of meeting face-to-face seemed both exciting and nerve-wracking. What would he think of me in person? Would the connection we shared online translate into real-life chemistry? These were questions that lingered in my mind, but they didn't dampen my curiosity or the growing sense that Randy was someone special.

Chapter 19: A Season of Change

As Logan and Daniel prepared to graduate, life began shifting in ways I hadn't fully anticipated. The boys were on the cusp of adulthood, ready to spread their wings, and with their newfound independence came decisions that would reshape all of our lives. It was a time of endings and new beginnings, a bittersweet transition that brought both pride and uncertainty.

Shortly before graduation, Daniel had gotten an old but impressive truck. It was the kind of vehicle that suited him perfectly, rugged, reliable, and full of character. He was a good driver, and the truck gave him a newfound sense of freedom. With that mobility came a decision that, while understandable, left me feeling a little wistful: Daniel decided to move back in with his mom.

I don't remember all the details, but I knew that this was something Daniel needed to do. He packed up his things, including his bedroom furniture, and set off for the next chapter of his life. It was a poignant moment, watching someone I had come to think of as a bonus child strike out on his own. I was proud of him, even as I felt the quiet ache of his absence.

Logan, too, was ready to chart his own course. He and his girlfriend, his prom date, decided to move back to Southeast Florida. It was a big step, but one that felt right for him at the time. As much as I wanted to hold on to the days when he was still under my roof, I knew it was time to let him go and find his own way.

With both boys leaving, the condo no longer made sense. I made the decision not to renew the lease and began the process of packing up and moving out. It was a whirlwind of activity: Logan and his girlfriend leaving for Florida, Daniel moving to his mother's house, and me sorting through what to keep, sell, and store.

I sold some furniture, put the rest in storage, and temporarily moved into the lake house. The quiet of those couple of weeks by the water gave me time to reflect on all the changes happening around me. The house, the boys, the life I had built in Fairfield Bay, it was all shifting, leaving me with the sense that it was time to move forward as well.

As my funds dwindled and work in rural Arkansas remained elusive, I found myself facing the question of what came next. Once again, my brother stepped in with an offer I couldn't refuse. He was working on a project in Memphis and needed help. It was the lifeline I needed, a chance to rebuild, refocus, and find a new purpose.

Grateful for the opportunity, I packed up my things and left Arkansas behind, heading back to Memphis. It wasn't just a move, it was a fresh start, a chance to rediscover who I was and what I wanted from life. Though the transitions were bittersweet, they were also necessary, marking the end of one chapter and the beginning of another.

Chapter 20: Landing at Akerswood

As the chapters of my life shifted again, I realized I needed a place to land, somewhere I could regroup and figure out my next steps. Naturally, I called Cindy, my best friend since high school, and asked if I could stay with her at Akerswood in Germantown, just outside of Memphis. Without hesitation, she eagerly said yes, reminding me yet again why she had been such an unwavering presence in my life.

Cindy isn't just a friend; she is family in every way that matters. We have shared a bond since high school, one that had weathered the many ups and downs of our lives. Over the years, she had been a constant in my ever-changing world, offering a voice of reason when my own thoughts became too chaotic. Her practicality, wisdom, and unwavering support made her someone I could always turn to, no matter the circumstance.

Her family was like an extension of mine. Cindy had been included in countless family events in Memphis, and I had known her parents for nearly 40 years by this point. Staying with Cindy wasn't just a matter of finding a place to stay, it was about finding a safe harbor with someone who knew and understood me on a profound level.

Packing my essentials into a bag, I left Arkansas behind and made my way to Memphis, grateful for Cindy's open door. Akerswood was a cozy and welcoming place, a perfect refuge during this transitional phase. Cindy made me feel immediately at home, as she always did, and her calm presence helped steady me in a time of uncertainty.

Though I intended to find my own place soon, having Cindy's support gave me the space to think clearly and plan my next steps. We spent our evenings catching up, laughing, and reminiscing about the adventures and misadventures of our shared history. She reminded me of who I was at my core and gave me the encouragement I needed to embrace this next chapter.

Throughout our adult lives, Cindy and I had remained in near-daily contact, even when miles separated us. She had always been a grounding force, someone who could offer advice without judgment and listen without interruption. In my chaotic world, Cindy was a lifeline, and her ability to bring clarity to even the most confusing situations was nothing short of a gift.

This chapter in Germantown wasn't just about a place to stay; it was about reconnecting with a friendship that had stood the test of time and leaning on someone who truly understood me. Cindy reminded me that even when life felt uncertain, I was never alone.

Chapter 21: Meeting Randy

The move to Memphis opened a door I had been waiting to walk through, the opportunity to meet Randy in person. After nearly a year of online conversations, Randy and I finally met face-to-face. From the very beginning, it was clear we had a connection that went beyond the screen. There was an ease to our interactions, a natural rhythm that made me want to explore this relationship further.

A few days after we met in person, I invited Randy to join me at the gym. It felt like the perfect way to spend time together, doing something I enjoyed while getting to know him better. After lifting weights, we transitioned to the indoor track. As we walked, I glanced out the window and noticed something familiar, the hospital where my aunt had worked as the director of the emergency room years ago.

I casually mentioned it to Randy, and to my surprise, he stopped dead in his tracks. He had worked at that very hospital as an emergency room attendant during his first job. It was a moment of serendipity that added a new layer of connection between us. The coincidence felt meaningful, as if the universe was aligning our paths. My aunt was his first boss in his first job.

As my initial project with my brother in Memphis came to an end, he approached me with another opportunity. He and his business partner, John, were opening a convenience store, gas station, and grill on Riverside Drive in downtown Memphis, and they needed my help. The idea intrigued me, and before long, we had the store up and running. Somehow, I ended up as the manager.

The Riverside Grill wasn't just any gas station, it was a hub of activity and, thanks to John's vision, a place where food was the star. The kitchen featured a hot box, a flat-top griddle, and a small menu of daily entrees, sides, and the best burgers in town, all made using John's recipes.

Across the street, a high-rise condo construction site ensured a steady stream of hungry customers. Every day, when the lunch whistle blew, the construction workers would march across the street in mass, forming a line at the grill and hot box. We served around 100 or more workers daily, dishing up meals that were simple but made with care.

By this time, Randy and I had only spent a handful of times together. Between my long hours managing the grill and his job, our schedules didn't always align. Then, one particularly busy lunch rush, amidst the chaos of flipping burgers and taking orders from the crowd of hungry construction workers, I glanced up, and there was Randy.

He had driven 30 minutes from his office to downtown Memphis, just to say hi during his lunch break. In the middle of the bustling store, surrounded by the noise of orders and sizzling food, his presence felt like a calm in the storm. I was elated to see him, and at that moment, something clicked. This wasn't just a fleeting connection or a casual relationship. Randy's effort, thoughtfulness, and willingness to make time for me spoke volumes.

That moment at Riverside Grill stayed with me. It wasn't just about Randy showing up, it was about what it symbolized. He wasn't just a passing ship in the night; he was someone who wanted to be a part of my life in a meaningful way. As I reflected on that day, I found myself growing increasingly excited about what the future might hold for us.

The grill, the chaos of the lunch rush, and the moments of connection with Randy all became intertwined in my mind, representing a time of change, hope, and the promise of something new.

Chapter 22: A Wake-Up Call

By this time, my parents had left their long-time Memphis home and settled into a picturesque retirement community on a freshwater lake called Miramar Lakes, just south of Fort Myers, Florida. Their new life was a stark contrast to the chaos that soon demanded my attention when I received a call from my mother, a call no parent wants to hear. My son, Logan, was in jail.

My mother's voice carried a mix of urgency and resolve as she explained the situation. Logan had been arrested in Fort Lauderdale on drug-related charges and disorderly conduct. She had already contacted her cousin, Jimmy, an attorney in Miami, to start working on getting Logan released on bail. But she had also decided that I needed to be there, and without waiting for my input, she booked me a flight to Florida. Her no-nonsense approach was clear: we were going to get to the bottom of this.

Later that afternoon, I boarded a plane bound for Florida. The weight of the situation pressed heavily on my mind. As much as I tried to prepare myself for what lay ahead, I knew I wouldn't fully understand the scope of the problem until I saw Logan and his surroundings for myself.

The next morning, my mother and I began the drive from her home in Miramar Lakes to Hollywood Beach, a bustling beachside town near Fort Lauderdale where Logan was living. The route took us across Alligator Alley, a stretch of highway cutting through the Everglades, and the drive gave us plenty of time to talk and reflect. Over coffee that morning, we had

Doug Ballinger Jr.

reviewed what little information we had, trying to piece together the details of Logan's situation.

Hollywood Beach was a far cry from the serene retirement community of Miramar Lakes. Logan's small apartment was located above a row of retail shops on a tourist-heavy strip, a lively and chaotic area that reflected the turmoil in his life.

As we neared Fort Lauderdale, Jimmy called my mother to let us know that Logan was being released from jail. The timing was uncanny; by the time we arrived at his apartment, we had barely parked before Logan pulled up a few spaces down from us.

The look on his face when he saw me and his grandmother standing there was unforgettable, a mix of shock, embarrassment, and a hint of relief. His clothes were disheveled, and he still carried the weight of the experience in his demeanor. Without much fanfare, he led me upstairs to his apartment while my mother waited in the car.

The moment I stepped into Logan's apartment, I was struck by its state of utter disarray. It was a far cry from the vibrant, independent life he had envisioned for himself. The space was in complete shambles, and it was clear that it had been a gathering place for his so-called friends, a drug flophouse, to put it bluntly. Empty bottles, scattered belongings, and the remnants of poor choices littered the space.

His girlfriend had already moved out by this point, leaving behind an atmosphere of abandonment and neglect. I suspected that the others who frequented the apartment were still in jail, leaving Logan to face the wreckage of his life alone.

Standing there, surveying the mess and the reality of Logan's situation, my heart broke for him. This wasn't the life I had imagined for my son, and it was clear that he was spiraling. But I also knew that this could be a turning point, a chance to pull him back from the edge if only he was willing to let me help.

Though the circumstances were dire, I resolved not to dwell on the mistakes that had led him here. Instead, I focused on what needed to happen next: getting Logan the support he needed and helping him clean up the physical and metaphorical mess in his life.

Chapter 23: Facing SUD and the Lies

It was during this difficult period with Logan that I came to a heartbreaking realization: he was in the grip of substance use disorder, actively battling addiction. The signs had been there, but like so many others who love someone struggling with addiction, I had been unable, or unwilling, to see them for what they were. My father, too, had been deceived, paying Logan's rent, fictitious college tuition, and providing spending money under the belief that Logan was working toward a brighter future. When the truth came out, my father was understandably angry, feeling betrayed and manipulated. It was a painful wake-up call for all of us.

Addiction doesn't just destroy the life of the person who is using, it creates a ripple effect, affecting everyone who loves and supports them. One of the most insidious aspects of addiction is the way it enables those who suffer from it to become master manipulators. In the early stages, many suffering with SUD become skilled at covering up their addiction, using excuses, fabricated stories, and appeals to emotion to maintain the facade that everything is fine.

Someone suffering with SUD are often adept at creating plausible narratives to explain away missing money, erratic behavior, or declining health. They might attribute these issues to stress, work pressures, or personal struggles, convincing their loved ones that they just need a little help to get back on track.

Someone suffering with SUD know how to exploit the unconditional love of their families and friends. They appeal to their loved ones' sense of hope, often promising that they're about to turn a corner, that they've hit rock bottom and will change if only they get this one last chance.

The stigma surrounding addiction makes it even easier for someone suffering with SUD to hide their struggles. They may lean into societal expectations, pretending to be high-functioning or even thriving, while concealing the reality of their situation.

Society's views on addiction remain one of the biggest barriers to addressing the crisis effectively. Far too often, addiction is seen not as a disease but as a moral failing, a lack of willpower, or evidence of bad choices. This stigma perpetuates harmful myths and discourages those struggling from seeking the help they need.

Like Logan many people struggling with addiction hide their struggles because of the shame associated with the label of "addict." They fear judgment, rejection, and the loss of dignity in the eyes of their community, friends, or family.

Addiction is a chronic disease that alters brain chemistry and impairs judgment and impulse control. Yet, society often blames individuals for their addiction, ignoring the biological, psychological, and social factors that contribute to substance use disorder.

The stigma creates a vicious cycle: someone suffering with SUD doesn't seek help because of fear and shame, and their condition worsens as a result. In turn, their worsening addiction reinforces negative stereotypes, perpetuating the belief that addiction is hopeless.

Overcoming the stigma of SUD requires a shift in how society views and addresses substance use disorder. It starts with education, empathy, and systemic change. My challenge to all of us is as follows:

- Our society must begin to teach that SUD is a disease, not a choice. Brain imaging studies have shown that addiction changes the brain's structure and function, particularly in areas related to decision-making, impulse control, and reward.

- We must normalize conversations about addiction in schools, workplaces, and communities to reduce the fear and shame surrounding the topic.

- We must practice compassion when interacting with someone who is struggling. Recognize that their behavior stems from a disease, not a lack of morals or effort.

- We must begin to offer support to those suffering from SUD and loved ones of addicts, who often suffer quietly and feel isolated due to societal judgment.

- We must advocate for comprehensive treatment options, including therapy, medication-assisted treatment, and long-term recovery programs. As well as expand access to affordable, evidence-based care, particularly in underserved communities where addiction often thrives due to lack of resources.

- We must continue to create support networks for those in recovery, offering mentorship, accountability, and opportunities to rebuild their lives.
- One of the most important issues is to celebrate stories of recovery to demonstrate that overcoming addiction is possible and worth pursuing.
- Use person-first language, such as "person with a substance use disorder" rather than "addict," to reduce stigma and humanize the individual.
- Avoid judgmental phrases like "clean" or "dirty," which carry moral connotations, and instead focus on supportive terms like "in recovery."

Logan's battle with addiction was a stark reminder of the complexities of substance use disorder. While it was painful to acknowledge the depth of his struggles, it also illuminated the need for compassion, education, and systemic change. Addiction can touch anyone, regardless of background, and the journey to recovery is rarely a straight path. But with the right support, understanding, and resources, RECOVERY IS POSSIBLE, not just for the individual, but for their family and community as well.

Chapter 24: A Fresh Start in Memphis

After Logan's legal troubles were resolved, thanks to the tireless efforts of our cousin Jimmy, it was clear that changes needed to be made. The decision was made for Logan to move back to Memphis, where I, along with the support of my brother, could keep a closer eye on him. With this move, Logan was given the opportunity to reset his life and begin to rebuild.

Back in Memphis, Logan found a sense of purpose working for my brother's gas station business again. He had a natural talent for car repairs and oil changes, and he quickly earned a reputation for being skilled and reliable. It was heartening to see him thrive in this environment, using his abilities to make a name for himself within the company.

Logan also secured a small apartment and, true to his nature, found himself in a relationship. For reasons I never fully understood, Logan always seemed to need a girlfriend, perhaps as a way to feel grounded or validated. While this pattern sometimes caused friction, it was part of who he was, and we worked around it as best as we could.

November of 2009 brought a joyous occasion: the 50th wedding anniversary of my parents, Gran and Granddaddy. My mother, in her inimitable style, orchestrated what felt like her own "going away party." It was a night filled with love, laughter, and memories, one that would remain etched in the hearts of everyone who attended.

The celebration was held at the Beach Club at Miramar Lakes, a venue befitting the grandeur of the occasion. It was a gathering of family and friends, some of whom hadn't seen each other in years but came together as though no time had passed. The evening was a blend of shared stories, heartfelt toasts, and the joy of being surrounded by loved ones.

The highlight of the night came toward the end, as the crowd moved to the beach. In a stunning tribute to my parents, their friends from Miramar Lakes organized a 15-minute fireworks display over the lake. The bright colors reflected on the water, painting the night sky with brilliance, perfectly capturing the magic and charm of the life my mother and father had built in this community.

Gran, even after just five years in Miramar Lakes, had made her mark. She was larger than life, and her presence left a lasting impression on everyone she met. It was clear where Logan got his grand sense of self; he carried a piece of his grandmother's charisma in his own personality.

As expected, Logan insisted that his girlfriend attend the anniversary celebration, despite some reservations from the family. Her presence caused a bit of friction here and there, but overall, the night remained focused on celebrating Gran and Granddaddy's milestone. It was a testament to the family's ability to come together, setting aside differences for the sake of love and unity.

The 50th-anniversary celebration wasn't just a tribute to Gran and Granddaddy's enduring love; it was a reminder of the bonds that tied our family together. The fireworks, the laughter, the shared meals, it all added up to a magical evening that honored their charmed life and the legacy they had created.

For Logan, it was another chance to reconnect with the family and see the strength of the relationships around him. For me, it was a moment to reflect on the ups and downs of life and to find hope in the way our family came together to celebrate something so beautiful.

Chapter 25: A Modern Christmas

Back in Memphis, Christmas that year felt a little different, a blend of tradition, technology, and adapting to new circumstances. My brother, JD, hosted the family gathering at his house in Memphis, creating a warm and festive atmosphere despite one significant absence: my parents. They joined us, however, in the next best way, via video call.

My mother hadn't been feeling well and chose not to travel, not wanting to risk catching a bug during the holiday season. It was a sensible decision, though her absence was felt. Thanks to technology, she and my father were able to join us virtually. It wasn't quite the same as having them there in person, but seeing their faces and hearing their voices during the celebration brought comfort and a sense of connection.

In many ways, it was ahead of its time, like an early version of today's common virtual gatherings on platforms like Skype or Zoom. We laughed and joked, passing the phone or laptop around so everyone could say hello and wish them a Merry Christmas.

JD's house was alive with holiday spirit, filled with family and close friends. Randy was there, adding his quiet but steady presence to the mix, as well as Cindy, always a source of light and laughter. A few other family friends joined the celebration, making it a lively and joyful occasion.

The day unfolded with the usual trappings of Christmas: opening presents, eating delicious food, and indulging in a bit of holiday cheer. JD's hosting skills shone through, creating an environment where everyone felt at ease and welcomed. The house rang with laughter and the sounds of holiday music, blending seamlessly with the warmth of conversation and the clinking of glasses.

The holidays came and went with a sense of quiet contentment. While life was always moving and changing, there was a shared understanding that everyone was doing well and moving forward in their own way. It was a time to reflect on the challenges of the past year, to celebrate the progress that had been made, and to look ahead with hope for what was to come.

Christmas that year was a reminder that while traditions evolve and circumstances shift, the essence of the holiday remains the same: the opportunity to come together, share love and laughter, and hold close the people who matter most, whether in person or across the miles.

Chapter 26: A Call That Changed Everything

If I had known what was coming, I would have done everything in my power to rewrite the script. I would have insisted on gathering our family and loved ones at my parents' home in Miramar Lakes for Christmas of 2009, celebrating one last perfect holiday with my mother and father. But life doesn't grant us the gift of foresight, and by the second week of March 2010, the world as I knew it began to unravel.

It started with a call that my mother had been taken to the hospital. She was struggling to breathe, a symptom that had grown increasingly common as her health deteriorated. My mother had battled a lifetime of health issues, and the toll was now impossible to ignore. Emphysema, congestive heart failure, and chronic anemia had all converged, leaving her body frail and her prognosis grim.

Despite the gravity of the situation, hope lingered. My brother JD and I held on to the possibility that she might pull through, as she had so many times before. We discussed traveling to Florida, but each time, there seemed to be some chance, however small, that she might turn a corner. That hope kept us rooted where we were, trying to believe in her resilience.

My mother had been pragmatic about her health for years, and her living will reflected that. It stated clearly: Do Not Resuscitate. Do Not Intubate. She had been explicit about her wishes to avoid extraordinary measures, and our family respected her decisions.

But then came the day when those wishes changed. In a moment of vulnerability and desperation, she allowed the doctors to intubate her. It was a sign that the situation had grown far worse than any of us had realized. My brother and I knew, without hesitation, that it was time to go to Florida. The call we dreaded had come: we needed to be there, now.

The decision to leave was immediate, but the weight of what we were walking into was crushing. JD and I prepared to travel, each of us silently grappling with what lay ahead. The road to Florida wasn't just a physical journey, it was a mental and emotional one, filled with unanswered questions and unspoken fears.

Would we make it in time? What would we find when we arrived? The thoughts churned as the miles stretched before us. This wasn't just a trip to see our mother, it was a reckoning with the inevitable, an acknowledgment that the center of our family might soon be gone.

As JD and I made our way to Miramar Lakes, the gravity of the situation began to settle in. My mother, the strong, spirited woman who had shaped so much of our lives, was slipping away. Her health had been a tenuous thread for years, but this time, the thread was unraveling faster than any of us could mend it.

There was no turning back, no way to change the course of events. All we could do was be there, for her, for our father, and for each other. The days ahead would test us in ways we couldn't yet imagine, but we were determined to face them together.

Chapter 27: The Drive to Goodbye

Packing for this journey felt surreal, like preparing for a trip you don't want to take but know you must. I packed a bag for myself and one for Hanz, my dog, and headed to Randy's house to spend the night. Randy lived close to JD, and since my brother and I planned to leave for Florida before sunrise, it made sense to stay there.

But sleep didn't come easily. As I lay there, staring into the darkness, my mind raced with thoughts of what was to come. How was I going to face the death of my mother, the woman who had been my guiding light all my life? The inevitability of it pressed on me like a weight I couldn't shift. This moment had always loomed in the distant future, but now it was rushing at us, unstoppable and unrelenting.

At some point, I must have fallen asleep, but in the still hours of the night, I awoke suddenly, startled and wide-eyed. Randy, stirred by my abrupt movement, looked at me with concern. I didn't have the words to explain what had just happened, I swore I heard music as clear as if it were playing on a stereo. The song was unmistakable: Temporary Home by Carrie Underwood.

The lyrics were like a direct message, carrying a strange sense of comfort amidst the alarm it brought. It felt as though my mother herself had sent the song to me, letting me know she was leaving her physical body and offering reassurance that this was not the end. It was a moment of connection, unexplainable yet deeply profound, and it calmed something inside me as I lay back down.

Before the sun rose, JD arrived to pick me up. I hugged Randy and Hanz goodbye, unsure of when I'd see them next, and climbed into the car with my brother. The drive to Florida stretched out ahead of us, one straight shot to Miramar Lakes. Neither of us wanted to make the trip, but there was no avoiding it now.

The car was filled with a heavy silence punctuated by occasional conversations. We talked a little about what lay ahead, but mostly we stayed quiet, each lost in our own thoughts. I chain-smoked cigarettes and gulped down coffee, trying to keep my nerves in check. The miles ticked by as we moved steadily closer to the inevitable.

Part of me couldn't help but wonder if my mother's decision to allow intubation had been a conscious choice to buy a little more time, a chance to see her children one last time. It seemed like something she would do, always thinking of her family first. Whether it was intentional or not, she had brought us together for this final chapter.

We reached Miramar Lakes in the early evening, exhausted but resolute. After a quick shower to wash away the road's grime, we headed to the hospital. I tried to prepare myself for what I might see, but nothing could have readied me for the sight of my mother strapped to that mobility bed in the ICU. Tubes and wires connected her to machines, and a bottle of propofol hung from a rack alongside other intravenous medications.

My brother and I approached her bedside, speaking to her softly, but there was no response. Her body was there, but her spirit seemed already far away. It was the first time I truly felt the weight of what was coming. She had always been the matriarch, the glue that held our family together. She was Logan's fiercest cheerleader, my biggest supporter, and JD's compass in times of doubt.

Standing there, powerless to change what was happening, the reality of her mortality was crushing. My mother, the vibrant, indomitable force who had shaped our lives, was nearing the end of her story. There was nothing we could do but be there, bearing witness to her final chapter and finding solace in the love and legacy she had left behind.

Family ties ran deep in Florida, where my mom's only sister, Annie, and her husband, Uncle Walt, had followed my parents to settle near them. The two couples shared a close bond, their lives intertwined in ways that brought both joy and comfort. On that Thursday night, Annie and Uncle Walt were at the hospital when JD and I arrived, their presence a reflection of the love and loyalty that defined our family.

When we arrived at the ICU, Annie was seated quietly, reading her Bible. She looked up, her face lined with the same mix of sorrow and resolve that JD and I felt. If anyone could understand the enormity of this loss, it was her, my mother's sister, her lifelong companion and confidante. Though she didn't say much, her silent presence spoke volumes. Like us, she was grappling with the reality that my mother, our family's guiding star, was slipping away.

My mother had always been "large and in charge," a force of nature who commanded every room and shaped the lives of everyone in her orbit. It was impossible to imagine a world without her. And yet, there we were, bracing ourselves for the inevitable.

That night, we left the hospital knowing what the next day would bring. We needed rest, but we also needed to face the practicalities of what was about to happen. My father, ever the steady anchor, took JD and me to a quiet restaurant for a discussion we couldn't avoid. Sitting there at the table, the three of us spoke as openly and frankly as possible about the end of a woman who had been a great wife, an amazing mother, and an even more incredible grandmother.

The topic of cremation came up. My mother had made her wishes abundantly clear over the years: she did not want her body taken back to New Madrid, Missouri, and buried. She'd always joked, half seriously, that she would haunt every one of us if we went against her wishes. None of us wanted to risk that, so we agreed. Cremation was not only practical; it was what she had wanted.

The atmosphere at the table was somber but united. As much as we hated losing her, we dreaded even more the task of telling our children what was about to happen. This wasn't just our loss; it was theirs too, and the weight of that responsibility was immense.

I don't remember what I ate that night, if I ate at all. The details of the meal have faded, but the memory of sitting at that table, speaking in hushed tones with my father and brother, remains vivid. It was a moment of clarity amidst the chaos, a rare instance where we could share our thoughts without the distractions of machines and hospital staff.

After dinner, we returned to my parents' house to rest. The hospital had my aunt's phone number and my father's number in case anything happened during the night. Despite the physical exhaustion from the drive and the emotional toll of the day, sleep did not come easily. The thought of what awaited us the next morning loomed large, pressing down on my chest like a weight that wouldn't lift.

The night was quiet, but not peaceful. Each of us was left to wrestle with our own thoughts, memories, and fears. My mother had been the glue that held our family together, the force that propelled us forward and gave us direction. And now, we were preparing to lose her. The reality of her absence felt incomprehensible, a void that would change everything.

It was around 1:00 in the morning when my phone rang. Somehow, I had managed to fall asleep despite the weight of the situation pressing on me, but the sound jolted me awake. The call was from my Annie. The hospital had tried to contact my father, but he hadn't answered, so they had reached out to her instead. She told me there had been a "neurological event", a term that felt cold and clinical at the moment, and that we needed to get to the hospital immediately. She and Uncle Walt were already on their way.

I threw on clothes and raced into the hallway, shouting for JD to wake up. My voice felt loud and jarring in the quiet of the night as I crossed the house to my father's room. He had found some semblance of sleep but woke quickly when I told him about the call. He jumped out of bed, dressed swiftly, and we left the house without hesitation.

I rode with my father while JD followed in his Suburban. The drive was silent except for the sound of my father praying softly, his words a quiet murmur in the stillness of the car. I didn't say much; I didn't know what to say. The urgency of the moment had wrapped me in a kind of numbness.

We arrived at the hospital at the same time as Annie and Walt, and together, we walked down the long corridor leading to the ICU. The sterile environment seemed colder than ever. At the nurses' station, we were met by a doctor and nurses who began to explain the situation. My mother had suffered some type of catastrophic neurological event. They told us that her chances of recovery were less than 2%.

Across from the nurses' station, I could see into my mother's ICU room through the sliding glass doors. Her body lay still on the bed, hooked up to the machines keeping her alive, the bed continuing its slow, methodical rotation. It was a heartbreaking sight, my vibrant, commanding mother reduced to this unresponsive state.

My father began looking at each of us, seeking consensus, as if he needed reassurance that he wasn't alone in what had to be done. I spoke up, my voice trembling but firm. "I think it's time to let her go. She's not coming back. She wouldn't want to be kept alive this way. We need to let her go and enjoy eternity with the God she served so well in her lifetime."

The room fell silent for a moment, then nods of agreement followed. Everyone knew it was the right decision, as painful as it was. My father signed the necessary paperwork, his hand steady but his heart surely breaking.

We each said our goodbyes. My father and JD chose to walk down the hall during the process, unable to witness what was about to happen. Annie and I stayed behind, determined to be with her as she passed. The nurses came in and gently explained what would happen, preparing us for the sights and sounds we might experience as her body began to shut down. Their compassion in that moment was a small but profound comfort.

They removed the intubation tube and stopped all intravenous medications. The change was immediate. Her body seemed to release all the tension it had been holding, surrendering to the natural process of death. Annie and I held vigil, saying Hail Marys and reading from the Psalms. The room was quiet except for the faint hum of the machines being turned off.

In those final moments, I found myself looking for signs of her spirit. I opened one of her eyelids, hoping for some flicker of recognition, a final glimpse of the mother I knew. I looked around the room, searching above the bed, wondering if I might see her essence leaving her body. But there was nothing, just the stillness of her earthly form, now free from the pain and struggles of life.

My mother had just died. The woman who had been my guiding light, my anchor, and the center of our family was gone.

Her story, so vibrant and full, had reached its final chapter.

We left the hospital in the still hours of the night, numb and hollow. My mother, our guiding light, our matriarch, was gone. As the reality settled in, the weight of her absence became almost unbearable. Outside in the parking lot, I had a brief moment where it all came crashing down, a small come apart. But I quickly pulled myself together. There were things to do, people to call, and a lifetime of connections to inform of her passing.

JD and I began making phone calls. JD called his daughters, Callie and Elizabeth, while I called Logan. Telling Logan that his grandmother was gone was one of the hardest conversations I've ever had. Other family members and friends were informed, and soon a wave of love and support began moving toward Miramar Lakes.

Arrangements were made for Logan, Callie, and Elizabeth to travel to Florida for the memorial service we planned for the following week. But, true to form, Logan deviated from the plan. Instead of traveling with his cousins, he arrived separately, with a girlfriend in tow. While it might have annoyed me under different circumstances, at that moment, I didn't have the emotional bandwidth to let it affect me. My mother was gone, and that overshadowed everything else.

Back at my parents' home, the house quickly filled with family and friends. People who had loved my mother, been influenced by her, and shared pieces of her remarkable life all came together to grieve, reminisce, and celebrate her legacy. Stories were told and retold, laughter mingling with tears as we tried to process the loss of such a vibrant and commanding presence.

A video montage was created for the memorial service, featuring pictures that captured her life and the love she had given to so many. Large photos were mounted and displayed around the house, reminders of her radiance and the moments that had defined her life. It was a bittersweet process, equal parts painful and cathartic.

Amidst the chaos of planning, a delivery arrived: a bouquet of at least three dozen white roses. They were stunning, taking up the entire wet bar area near the kitchen. Each time I walked by them, I couldn't help but think how beautiful they were. In the haze of everything else, I didn't immediately check the card, but the roses stood as a silent reminder of love and support.

When I finally read the card, it left me speechless: God bless Mary Elizabeth and everyone who loved her. Signed, Randy.

It was a gesture that hit me like a wave. Even though Randy couldn't be there, he had sent this beautiful token of care and thoughtfulness. The moment I read the card, I called him, overcome with gratitude. His thoughtfulness meant so much at a time when everything felt unmoored.

The first memorial service was held at the church my parents had supported and loved in Florida. It was a full house, filled with people who had been touched by my mother's life. Logan's mom, Gina, even traveled from Sarasota to be there, a testament to the respect and love my mother had inspired in everyone she met.

Plans were also made, though I wasn't involved in the decision, for a second memorial service in Memphis the following week. While I understood the reasoning, it was emotionally exhausting. It felt like ripping the Band-Aid off twice, leaving little room to begin the healing process.

In a moment of levity, and perhaps a need to escape the heaviness of grief, my father decided to take all of us to a three-ring circus set up nearby. It was an unexpected choice, but in a strange way, it worked. The laughter, the spectacle, and the surreal distraction of the circus tent offered a brief reprieve from the sorrow.

The following day, we prepared to leave Florida and head back to Memphis. The house was straightened up, cars were packed, and we caravanned back, six cars of family and friends making the journey together. My father joined us, a man who seemed both lost and quietly at peace with the idea that my mother had reached her destiny.

Chapter 28: Intervention at Cindy's

A few years before my mother passed away, Logan's addiction surfaced again in a way we couldn't ignore. He had been working at one of my brother JD's gas stations, a job we hoped would give him structure and purpose. But then JD discovered that money was missing, more than just a little. The sum was substantial enough that there was no denying the gravity of the situation. JD and I had a serious conversation about what had happened. We both suspected that Logan was using drugs again, and we knew we needed to address the issue head-on.

We made a plan to confront him, not with anger or accusations but with love and concern. We wanted Logan to know that we were on his side and that our goal wasn't to punish him but to help him find a way out of the spiral he was in. We decided to hold the conversation at my best friend Cindy's house, a neutral and safe place where Logan wouldn't feel cornered.

The three of us, JD, Cindy, and I, waited for Logan to arrive. Each of us had known him since the day he was born, and he was special to all of us. Despite the seriousness of the situation, our love for him was unwavering. When Logan walked in, his guard was already up. He knew something was coming, and he took a defensive posture from the start, his body language screaming defiance even before we said a word.

We started gently, laying out the facts. Logan didn't deny taking the money. He admitted to using it to buy heroin but quickly followed up with claims that he hadn't used it recently. To prove his point, he began stripping off his clothes, showing us his arms and legs to demonstrate there were no fresh injection marks. It was a dramatic gesture, one that spoke volumes about the shame and desperation he carried beneath his bravado.

The conversation was long and difficult, oscillating between moments of tension and brief glimpses of connection. We talked about the money, the addiction, and the path his life was taking. Logan eventually dropped his defenses, and we got through to him. Reluctantly, he agreed to go to rehab.

JD had already researched a facility in East Tennessee that came highly recommended. We didn't want to give Logan time to change his mind, so JD immediately loaded him into the car and began the drive to East Tennessee. It was just days before Thanksgiving, and we knew that Logan would spend both Thanksgiving and Christmas in treatment. It wasn't an easy decision, but it was the best one we could make.

My mother wasn't thrilled about Logan being away for the holidays. She wanted him home, surrounded by family, but even she acknowledged that this was the right thing to do. The holidays were tough that year, marked by an undercurrent of worry and hope. We missed him terribly, but knowing he was in a safe place gave us some comfort.

Logan successfully completed the 30-day program and came back to Memphis. But I knew that being in the same environment, surrounded by the same triggers and enablers, would make it hard for him to stay on the right path. I talked to

Gina, his mother, about the possibility of him moving to Sarasota to live with her. She agreed it was a good idea and promised to encourage him to attend Narcotics Anonymous meetings and stay focused on his recovery.

It was another tough transition, but we all hoped that this move would give Logan the fresh start he needed. For the moment, it felt like we were moving in the right direction, and that was enough to hold onto.

Addiction doesn't just erode a person's health and happiness; it distorts their reality and relationships. To maintain their habit, someone suffering with SUD often become masters of deception, weaving intricate lies and manipulating those who care about them most. Logan was no exception. He had an uncanny ability to look you in the eye and tell you what you wanted to hear, often blending just enough truth into his stories to make them plausible. Whether it was explaining away missed work shifts or denying drug use, his words were carefully constructed shields meant to deflect suspicion and avoid accountability.

Someone suffering with SUD often employs tactics like denial, minimization, and projection to keep their addiction hidden. They'll downplay the seriousness of their situation "It's not that bad", shift blame onto others "If you weren't so controlling, I wouldn't need this", or claim they have it under control "I can quit whenever I want". Logan, like many others, used these strategies to convince us, and perhaps himself, that he didn't have a problem. His dramatic gesture of stripping off his clothes to prove he wasn't using heroin at that moment was a prime example. It wasn't about facing the root issue but about creating a diversion to avoid confronting the deeper truth.

Rehabilitation is often seen as a lifeline, but the road to recovery is anything but straightforward. According to data from the National Institute on Drug Abuse (NIDA), the relapse rate for substance use disorders is 40-60%, comparable to chronic diseases like diabetes and hypertension. These statistics highlight the challenges of addiction recovery and underscore why treatment needs to be comprehensive, ongoing, and individualized.

Too often, rehab programs are treated as a one-size-fits-all solution. A standard 30-day program might work for some, but for others, it's merely a starting point. Addiction rewires the brain, affecting decision-making, impulse control, and emotional regulation. Addressing these changes requires not just detoxification but also therapy, life skills training, and aftercare support.

Unfortunately, access to high-quality rehab is uneven. Many facilities focus more on detox and short-term care rather than providing the tools needed for long-term recovery. For Logan, the program in East Tennessee was a step in the right direction, but it wasn't enough on its own. He needed ongoing support, Narcotics Anonymous meetings, therapy, and a change in environment, to reinforce the progress he had made.

One of the most glaring issues with addiction treatment is the lack of attention paid to the quality and continuity of care. While there are exceptional programs, the system as a whole often falls short. Many rehabs lack sufficient funding, leading to understaffed facilities, limited therapeutic options, and outdated approaches. Others are prohibitively expensive, putting life-saving care out of reach for many families.

There's also a cultural stigma around seeking help, particularly for substance use disorders. Society often views addiction as a moral failing rather than a medical condition, which discourages people from reaching out. Even within the healthcare system, someone suffering with SUD are sometimes treated with judgment rather than compassion, further alienating them from the support they need.

Logan's experience highlighted these gaps. While we were fortunate to find a good facility for him, the burden of navigating his recovery largely fell on us as his family. We were left to cobble together a patchwork of solutions, hoping that they would hold. It's a common story for families grappling with loved ones in active addiction, a system that offers some help but not enough, leaving people to fight an uphill battle against a relentless disease.

Despite the grim statistics and systemic shortcomings, recovery is possible. Success often depends on a combination of factors: the individual's willingness to change, the quality of the treatment they receive, and the strength of their support network. For Logan, each attempt at rehab was a chance to plant seeds of hope, even if they didn't always take root right away. And for us, his family, every small step forward was a reminder that while the journey was hard, it was never without the possibility of redemption.

When Logan first moved to Florida, he seemed genuinely determined to turn his life around. Being with his mom gave him a sense of stability, and he assured both of us that he was attending Narcotics Anonymous (NA) meetings and doing his best to stay clean. For a while, it felt like we were on the right track.

But recovery is rarely a straight path. I'll never forget the conversation we had when I asked him why he stopped going to NA meetings. With striking clarity, he said, "Those meetings are the easiest place to find drug connections." His honesty hit hard, not just because of what it revealed about his struggles but because it highlighted a systemic issue in addiction recovery.

Support groups like NA or AA are cornerstones of recovery for many, offering community and accountability. But they also come with risks. For some participants, these groups can inadvertently serve as a place to meet individuals who are still actively using or who have access to substances. While most attendees are committed to recovery, the presence of even a few individuals who aren't focused can undermine the group's safety and purpose. For Logan, this risk outweighed the benefits, leading him to step away from a support system that might have helped him.

Addiction recovery programs, including 12-step meetings, often operate independently and rely heavily on peer leadership. While this structure fosters mutual support, it also lacks safeguards to ensure that the environment remains conducive to recovery. For individuals like Logan, who were actively seeking a drug-free lifestyle, the lack of oversight made it easy to encounter triggers in what should have been a safe space.

The "one-size-fits-all" approach to recovery doesn't account for individual needs and circumstances. Some people thrive in group settings like NA, while others, like Logan, find them counterproductive. Comprehensive recovery programs should offer a range of options, including one-on-one counseling, holistic therapies, and alternative peer support groups that better align with a person's personality and triggers.

Even when someone is willing to seek help, systemic barriers often make it difficult. High costs, limited insurance coverage, and a shortage of treatment programs are common hurdles. Additionally, many programs focus on short-term solutions like detox or 30-day rehab, without providing the long-term support needed for sustained recovery. For Logan, this lack of continuity in care meant that after his time in rehab, he was largely left to navigate recovery on his own.

The stigma surrounding addiction often discourages people from seeking or fully engaging with recovery programs. Those suffering with SUD are frequently seen as morally weak rather than individuals battling a chronic disease, leading to shame and isolation. This societal attitude permeates even the recovery community, where judgment can sometimes come from other participants or facilitators. For Logan, stigma likely played a role in his reluctance to re-engage with traditional recovery spaces after feeling they weren't helping him.

Addiction is rarely an isolated problem. It often stems from deeper issues like trauma, mental health challenges, or socioeconomic pressures. Effective recovery requires addressing these root causes, but many programs focus solely on stopping substance use without providing resources for broader healing. Logan's experience underscored this gap, while he may have temporarily stopped using, the deeper issues driving his addiction were never fully addressed.

For recovery systems to truly support those struggling with substance use disorder, several improvements are needed:

- Programs should tailor treatment plans to each individual's needs, including options beyond group meetings, such as intensive therapy, life skills training, and community-building activities that don't revolve around addiction.
- Recovery spaces need better safeguards to minimize exposure to triggers and prevent relapse.
- Recovery is a lifelong process. Programs should provide continuous care, including alumni networks, follow-up counseling, and resources to help individuals reintegrate into society.
- Addiction treatment must go beyond detox to tackle underlying issues like mental health, trauma, and socioeconomic instability.
- Society must shift its perception of addiction from a moral failing to a medical condition deserving empathy and support.

Logan's honesty about why he stopped attending NA meetings serves as a stark reminder that even well-intentioned systems can have flaws. His journey reflects the broader challenges faced by millions battling addiction: the need for more effective, compassionate, and comprehensive support.

Logan's move to Florida was meant to be a fresh start, a way to distance himself from the people and places that had fueled his addiction. For the most part, it worked, at least for a while. He seemed happy to be with his mom, and for a time, he was focused on staying clean. But recovery is never easy, and Logan often found himself grappling with challenges both external and internal.

One of those challenges was his mom's love of wine. Gina was, by all accounts, a wonderful mother and an extraordinary person, kind, loving, and supportive. But she enjoyed her wine, sometimes a bit too much, and it weighed heavily on Logan. He confided in me about it often, expressing how difficult it was to stay on track when alcohol was such a visible presence in the home. It wasn't that Gina didn't want to support Logan's recovery, she did, in every way she knew how, but the dynamic added an extra layer of complexity to an already difficult journey.

During this time, Logan seemed to find a sense of focus and purpose in his work as a bartender at the Chart House restaurant on Longboat Key. The restaurant business was in his blood; he had grown to love it and understood every nuance of the job. Logan excelled in this environment, thriving on the energy, the fast pace, and the opportunity to connect with people.

It was heartening to see him doing so well. He took pride in his work and enjoyed the camaraderie of his coworkers. Over the phone, he would tell me about his shifts, share funny stories from the restaurant, and talk about the people he met. Those daily conversations were a lifeline for both of us, a chance to stay connected despite the miles between us.

But addiction has a way of casting long shadows. During this period, Logan and a friend got into trouble for stealing some artwork and then destroying it to avoid getting caught. At the time, I had no idea this had happened. It wasn't until years later, after an unrelated automobile accident, that the full story came to light. This episode, like so many others, was a reminder of how addiction warps decision-making and leaves a trail of consequences that can linger for years.

Despite these setbacks, Logan was generally happy and doing well in recovery during this time. His phone calls were filled with optimism and plans for the future. We talked almost daily, and I cherished those conversations, they were a window into his world, a chance to share his victories and support him through his struggles.

Recovery is a journey marked by highs and lows, moments of clarity, and moments of relapse. Logan's time in Florida reflected all of this, the joy of finding purpose in his work, the pain of navigating complex family dynamics, and the constant battle to stay on the right path. Through it all, Logan remained my son, a person of immense heart and resilience, someone who never stopped trying to be better, even when the odds were stacked against him.

Chapter 29: A Season of Loss

Over the next few years, Logan's life was marked by profound changes and heartbreaking losses. He was living in Sarasota with his mom, Gina, and close to her parents, whom Logan had always adored. His grandmother, Grammy, was particularly special to him. She was a constant source of love and warmth, and Logan cherished the time they spent together.

When Grammy received a terminal diagnosis and was placed in hospice care, Logan's world shifted. He spent as much time as he could by her side, tending to her needs and showing her the deep respect and love she had always shown him. In those final weeks, Logan's quiet presence at her bedside was a testament to his compassion and ability to be fully present in moments of great emotional weight. Watching her slip away was devastating, and when she passed, Logan felt the heavy void of her absence. He had now lost both of his grandmothers, leaving an indelible mark on his heart.

Grammy's passing left her husband, Grandfather, alone for the first time in many decades. They had shared a lifetime together, and the loss of his wife was unbearable for him. Logan, sensing his grandfather's grief, spent much of his time with him in the months that followed. The two found solace in each other's company, sharing stories, meals, and quiet moments. For Logan, comforting his grandfather became a way to channel his own grief, and their bond grew even stronger during this time.

But grief has a way of creeping in when least expected. One day, Logan called me, his voice filled with shock and sadness. Someone had found Grandfather dead, and it appeared to be a suicide. There was a note, a final goodbye, and the overwhelming heartbreak of another loss. Logan had now faced the deaths of three pivotal figures in his life: both of his grandmothers and his grandfather. Each loss compounded the weight he carried, and now Grandfather, the man he had sought comfort from, was gone too.

Gina, grappling with her own grief, decided to make a fresh start. She moved to the Chicago area to be near a lifelong friend, securing a good job and a cozy apartment. It was a decision she needed to make for herself, but it meant that Logan was now largely on his own in Sarasota. While Gina's brothers, Kevin and Justin, were still in town and available in emergencies, Logan faced the reality of navigating life without the close familial support he had once relied on.

This new chapter was a test of Logan's resilience. Sarasota, once a place filled with family and familiarity, now felt emptier. The weight of these losses and the changes in his life became yet another layer in the complex journey of recovery and self-discovery he was on.

One of the many twists in Logan's journey came after a car accident that revealed more than just damage to his vehicle. He was hit by a woman driving a car from a used car lot, neither the driver nor the car was insured. The situation was frustrating and complicated, but my father, ever resourceful, enlisted an attorney friend to write a letter to the car lot owner, requesting compensation for Logan's repairs.

The response we received caught us off guard. The dealership's attorney rebutted our claim by bringing up Logan's past: his arrest and conviction for stealing artwork. It was a bombshell revelation, something Logan had worked hard to keep hidden from me and the rest of the family. I was angry and hurt, but I also had to admit a certain respect for how he had handled the legal fallout. Logan had navigated the consequences on his own, ensuring he paid his court-ordered restitution and avoided significant jail time. He never asked for help with his legal troubles, at least, not directly.

Over time, however, Logan did reach out for financial help to meet his restitution payments. I struggled with those requests. On one hand, I wanted to support him in fulfilling his obligations. On the other, I feared that giving him money would enable him to buy drugs. I resolved not to give him cash but instead made a few payments directly to the court on his behalf. Still, it was a difficult and imperfect solution. By covering his restitution, I might have freed up his earnings for other uses, including drugs. It was an impossible balancing act, and every decision felt like a gamble.

Parenting someone with a substance use disorder is one of the most gut-wrenching roles a person can have. The concept of tough love, withholding financial or emotional support to avoid enabling harmful behavior, is often touted as the "right" way to handle addiction. But in practice, it's far more nuanced and painful than any guideline or article can prepare you for.

The central tenet of tough love is to avoid enabling the behavior of someone suffering from SUD. This means not giving them money, shelter, or other resources that could indirectly support their addiction. But the line between helping and enabling is razor thin. For example, when I made those restitution payments for Logan, I believed I was helping him meet his obligations and avoid further legal trouble. Yet I couldn't ignore the possibility that, by easing his financial burden, I was indirectly enabling his addiction.

Every decision comes with a mix of guilt, worry, and self-doubt. When you refuse to give your child money, you wonder if you're pushing them further into desperation. When you help them, you fear you're contributing to their addiction. There's no escape from the emotional torment of questioning whether you're doing the right thing.

Some parents are advised to cut ties entirely, believing that an addict must hit rock bottom before they'll seek help. But as a parent, the thought of turning your back on your child is unbearable. What if this time is the one where they truly need you? What if the distance pushes them deeper into despair? Tough love may sound like a straightforward solution, but it's fraught with risks and uncertainties.

Finding the balance between support and accountability is perhaps the hardest part. You want to encourage your child's recovery and growth, but without shielding them from the consequences of their actions. For Logan, paying restitution was an essential step in taking responsibility for his past. By refusing to give him cash but making direct payments, I tried to walk that tightrope. Whether I succeeded is something I still wrestle with.

Tough love isn't just hard on the person with SUD, it's grueling for the family. It requires constant vigilance, difficult conversations, and decisions that haunt you long after they're made. For me, the process of saying "no" to Logan when I desperately wanted to say "yes" took a toll on my heart and my spirit. I wanted to trust him, to believe he was making progress, but the fear of relapse loomed over every interaction.

Through it all, I reminded myself that my love for Logan never wavered. Even when I had to make hard choices, it was always with his well-being in mind. Tough love isn't about withholding love; it's about expressing it in a way that prioritizes the person's long-term health and safety, even when it hurts.

Chapter 30: The Complex Role of Parenting Someone with a Substance Use Disorder (SUD)

Parenting is challenging under the best of circumstances. However, parenting someone with a substance use disorder (SUD) transforms those challenges into a relentless emotional and logistical battle. The role demands constant vigilance, extraordinary patience, and a deep well of compassion, even as it pushes parents to confront feelings of anger, betrayal, and helplessness.

For me, parenting Logan through his addiction meant navigating a labyrinth of difficult decisions. Each step felt like a minefield and every choice, whether to intervene, to give, to withhold, carried potential consequences that could either help or harm him. It was a journey of constant learning, deep heartache, and unwavering love.

The love for your child never diminishes, no matter how difficult their journey becomes. But addiction complicates that love, mixing it with feelings of frustration, fear, and even anger. Watching your child battle addiction is like watching them drown, reaching out for help one moment and pushing you away the next.

For parents, it's hard to reconcile the person they knew, the vibrant, hopeful child, with the version struggling with SUD. There were moments with Logan when I could still see glimpses of the boy I raised, and those moments gave me hope. But there were also times when his addiction made him a stranger, and those times broke my heart.

Every phone call became a source of anxiety. Was he okay? Was he in trouble? Was this going to be the call where I heard the worst news of all? The fear of losing Logan was ever-present, a shadow that followed me every day. It's a fear I know many parents of children with SUD share, a fear that is both suffocating and motivating.

As parents, we often ask ourselves, What did I do wrong? or Could I have done something differently? With addiction, these questions become even more pronounced. I found myself replaying moments from Logan's childhood, wondering if I had missed signs or made decisions that contributed to his struggles. While I know intellectually that addiction is a complex disease influenced by many factors, the emotional weight of guilt is hard to shake.

Effective parenting through SUD requires balancing accountability with support. It's about setting boundaries while reminding your child they are loved unconditionally. For me, this meant staying in regular contact with Logan, letting him know I was there for him emotionally, even if I couldn't give him money or solve every problem for him. It was a delicate dance of being firm yet compassionate, present yet careful not to enable.

Many parents struggle to find accessible, high-quality treatment for their children. Rehab programs can be prohibitively expensive, and affordable options often have long waitlists or inadequate services. When Logan needed help, I often felt like I was piecing together a patchwork of resources, none of which fully addressed his needs.

The stigma surrounding addiction affects not only the person struggling but also their family. As a parent, you may feel judged, as though your child's addiction is a reflection of your failure.

This stigma can make it hard to seek support, leaving many parents to navigate the journey in isolation.

When Logan faced legal consequences, I saw firsthand how the justice system often criminalizes addiction rather than treating it as a medical issue. Parents are left to advocate for their children in a system that rarely prioritizes recovery over punishment.

Chapter 31: Lessons Learned Along The Way

Through the ups and downs of Logan's journey, I've learned a few key lessons about parenting through SUD:

- You Can't Do It Alone. Seeking support, from therapists, support groups, or trusted friends, is essential. Addiction affects the whole family, and parents need care and guidance just as much as their children do.

- Recovery is a process, not a destination. Progress is rarely linear. There were times when Logan seemed to be doing well, only to fall back into old patterns. Each step forward, no matter how small, is worth celebrating.

- Love is always the foundation. No matter how hard things got, I never stopped loving Logan. That love was the foundation of every decision I made, even the tough ones.

- Forgive Yourself. Parents aren't perfect, and addiction is a complex disease with no single cause or solution. It's important to let go of the guilt and focus on doing the best you can at the moment.

Parenting someone with SUD is one of the hardest roles a person can take on, but it's also a profound act of love. Logan's journey taught me that while I couldn't fight his battles for him, I could walk beside him, offering support, hope, and unconditional love. That's what being his parent meant to me, even in the most challenging moments.

Chapter 32: The Juggling Act of Addiction

Addiction creates a fractured existence, forcing individuals to live in multiple worlds, each with its own demands and dynamics. For Logan, there were the familial relationships he worked to maintain, the professional world of the restaurant business where he excelled, and the shadowy sphere of addiction, with its dangerous entanglements and relentless pull.

To the outside world, Logan seemed to have it together. As a server, bartender, and front-of-house manager, he exuded charm and competence. He could light up a room, impress patrons, and cultivate the illusion of being in control. When we talked, Logan often shared stories of his work, the big tips he earned, the celebrities he met, the fancy dinners he served. He loved the rush of the restaurant business, the energy and validation it gave him. In his mind, he was a big shot, someone who had it all figured out. But beneath that facade was a young man grappling with the weight of addiction, juggling multiple lives while trying to hold everything together.

Living in these separate worlds required Logan to constantly compartmentalize. There was his family, me, Gina, and our families, where he needed to present himself as doing well, clean, and in control. Then there were his friends and coworkers, many of whom were likely unaware of the depths of his struggles. And finally, there was the world of addiction, where he navigated dangerous relationships with dealers and fellow users.

The pressure to keep these lives from colliding must have been immense. Addiction thrives on secrecy, and Logan was skilled at telling people what they wanted to hear. But the cracks inevitably showed. Whether it was through subtle signs of stress, moments of manipulation, or outright crises, the walls between his worlds were impossible to maintain indefinitely.

One day, Logan called me with a story that shook me to my core. He told me he needed $2,200 to pay off a drug dealer who, he claimed, had threatened to kill him if he didn't come up with the money. It was a desperate plea, and at the moment, I had no way of knowing whether the story was true or a fabrication to elicit help.

This is one of the cruelest aspects of addiction, it distorts trust and blurs the line between truth and manipulation. I knew Logan was always looking for an angle, and the possibility that he was reselling drugs to support his habit added another layer of uncertainty. Was he truly in danger, or was this just another attempt to fund his addiction? I'll never know.

When Logan called, panic and fear gripped me. The thought of my son being harmed was unbearable. But so was the idea of handing over money that could perpetuate his addiction or enable dangerous behavior. At that moment, I had to make one of the hardest decisions of my life. I told him, as calmly as I could, that the best I could offer was advice: find a good hiding spot. I didn't say it to be cruel; I said it because giving him money to pay off a drug dealer, or to buy drugs, was a line I couldn't cross. Even if it meant losing my son, I had to hold firm.

As a parent, this decision tore me apart. The instinct to protect your child is overwhelming, but addiction complicates everything. Helping doesn't always look like helping, and tough love doesn't always feel like love. I knew Logan would be angry, hurt, and maybe even terrified. But I also knew that giving in to his request could cause more harm in the long run.

Logan, like many suffering with SUD, was adept at creating stories to garner sympathy or assistance from those who loved him. Addiction doesn't just affect the person using, it pulls their entire support system into its orbit, forcing them to navigate a web of lies, manipulation, and emotional upheaval. The fear and desperation those in active addiction feel often drive them to say or do whatever it takes to secure their next fix, even if it means putting their relationships at risk.

This call was one of many moments where I had to confront the painful reality of Logan's addiction. It tested my resolve and forced me to wrestle with questions no parent should ever have to face: What if I refuse, and something happens to him? What if I give in, and it only makes things worse? How do I show love when every decision feels like it could backfire?

After that call, Logan was angry with me, and I understood why. In his eyes, I had abandoned him when he needed me most. But in my heart, I knew that giving him money wouldn't have solved anything. It would have been a temporary fix, one that likely would have deepened his struggles. Tough love is a painful road, filled with guilt, second-guessing, and heartbreak. But it's also rooted in hope, the hope that by holding firm, you're helping your child in the long run, even if they can't see it in the moment.

Looking back, I still wrestle with the decisions I made during Logan's addiction. There were no perfect answers, only imperfect choices made out of love and desperation. Addiction doesn't come with a manual, and every parent of a child suffering with SUD is forced to write their own playbook, balancing compassion with boundaries, and love with accountability.

Through it all, I never stopped loving Logan. Even in the hardest moments, my love for him was the constant thread that guided me. Addiction tried to pull us apart, but it could never break that bond. And while I couldn't always protect him from the dangers of his world, I could, and did, remind him every day that he was never alone.

Chapter 33: Logan, the Defender

Logan had a way of stepping into situations with a mix of charm, courage, and defiance that left an impact on everyone around him. He wasn't one to stand by and let someone be treated unfairly or left vulnerable, especially those he cared about. It didn't matter if it was a friend, a stranger, or, in this case, his young cousin. Logan always found a way to act, often with a fierce determination and a touch of rebelliousness.

Ashley shared a story about a family trip in May 2010, when Grammy and Grandfather treated their children and grandchildren to a four-night cruise to the Bahamas. It was the kind of trip that was meant to create lifelong memories, and Logan made sure one of those memories would be his act of kindness toward his cousin Caitlyn.

The family was enjoying a sunny day on Royal Caribbean's private island in the Bahamas. Ashley's daughter Caitlyn, just 16 months old at the time, had fallen asleep on a lounge chair. But there was no shade where they were sitting, and the baby was exposed to the intense island sun. It was one of those small moments where a problem arises, and most people might think, That's too bad. There's nothing I can do.

Not Logan. Without saying a word, he got up and set out to find a solution. He walked quite a distance to locate an umbrella, something no one else had thought to do, and brought it back to Caitlyn's chair. Sticking the umbrella in the sand, he created a patch of shade so she could nap comfortably and safely. For a moment, it seemed like the problem was solved.

Then, a staff member approached, telling the family that umbrellas weren't allowed in that section of the beach. It was one of those rigid rules that might make sense on paper but felt heartless in practice. Logan wasn't having it. He stood up for Caitlyn in a way only he could. With his trademark mix of charm and audacity, he told the staff member that Caitlyn, his 16month-old cousin, needed the shade to avoid overheating. "Are you really going to let her fry in the sun?" he asked, his voice full of conviction.

The staff member, perhaps recognizing the futility of arguing with Logan, walked away. The umbrella stayed, and Caitlyn enjoyed a peaceful, shaded nap thanks to her cousin's determination.

This story is quintessential Logan. It captures so much of who he was, his thoughtfulness, his willingness to act, and his ability to blend charm with defiance when the situation called for it. Logan didn't wait to be asked for help; he saw a need and stepped in, even if it meant bending a few rules along the way.

His actions on that beach reflect the same spirit he carried throughout his life. Logan was fiercely protective of the people he loved and always ready to stand up for what he thought was right, whether it was for a napping baby or someone facing an injustice. It wasn't about seeking attention or praise; it was about his innate sense of compassion and his determination to do the right thing, no matter the circumstances.

In sharing this story, Ashley highlighted a side of Logan that those who knew him will never forget. Even in the midst of his struggles, Logan's heart shone through in moments like these. It's these memories, the ones filled with love, kindness, and a touch of rebellion, that paint the full picture of who he was. Logan wasn't just someone who fought his own battles; he fought for others too, and he did it with a spirit that left a lasting impression on everyone he encountered.

Chapter 34: Parenting a Charming Addict

Parenting a child with substance use disorder (SUD) is like living in two worlds at once. On one hand, there's the love and pride you feel for the person they are, the charm, the intelligence, the humor, the glimpses of their potential when addiction doesn't overshadow it all. On the other hand, there's the constant pain and fear that comes with recognizing the reality of their addiction and its grip on their life.

Logan embodied this duality perfectly. He was a charmer, always able to light up a room and win people over. He had a knack for making people feel seen and valued, and his quick wit and warmth made him magnetic. Stories like the one Ashley shared about the Bahamas trip remind me that his charm wasn't just superficial, it came from a place of genuine care and compassion for others.

But addiction doesn't erase a person's best qualities; it complicates them. Logan's charm could also serve as a mask, a tool to deflect concern or manipulate situations to his advantage. As a parent, it was both a blessing and a burden to see him navigate these two worlds, one of success and potential, and one of addiction and struggle.

When Logan was thriving, working in a restaurant, managing his responsibilities, or showing his innate kindness, it was easy to hope. Those glimpses of success, however fleeting, became lifelines for me. They were reminders that he wasn't defined solely by his addiction, that the person I knew and loved was still there, fighting to break free.

Logan's charm played a role in these moments. He had a way of making you believe in him, of convincing you that he was on the right path. I clung to those moments, even when the signs of his addiction lingered in the background. As a parent, it's almost impossible not to. You want so desperately to believe that this time, things will be different. This time, they'll stay on track. This time, the addiction won't win.

But addiction is relentless, and the reality of it never stays hidden for long. For every moment of hope, there were moments of heartbreak, missed opportunities, relapses, and the lies that inevitably come with addiction. Logan's charm and charisma often made it hard to see the full picture. He could tell you what you wanted to hear, spinning stories that were almost believable, even when the truth was staring you in the face.

As a parent, recognizing the signs of addiction in someone so capable, so full of life, is a uniquely painful experience. It's a constant push and pull between hope and reality, between wanting to believe the best and bracing yourself for the worst.

The glimpses of success made it harder to fully confront the depth of Logan's struggles, and the depth of his struggles made those glimpses all the more precious.

There were moments when I had to remind myself that addiction is a disease, not a choice. Logan wasn't charming to manipulate me; he was using the tools he had to survive in a life that had become so much harder than it should have been. That understanding didn't make it easier, but it helped me stay grounded when the line between Logan the son I loved, and Logan the addict blurred.

Through it all, I learned that loving someone with SUD means embracing both realities, the charm and the addiction, the hope and the heartbreak. It means recognizing that your child is more than their disease, even when the disease feels all-consuming. It means holding onto those glimpses of success as reminders of their potential, while never losing sight of the work that still needs to be done.

Most importantly, it means loving them unconditionally, even when their actions hurt you. Logan's charm and kindness were as much a part of him as his addiction. They were reminders of who he was at his core, and they gave me hope, even in the darkest moments.

Chapter 35: The Call That Changed Everything

The dawn of 2020 came with the looming specter of COVID19, a threat that would soon reshape the world in unimaginable ways. But for our family, the year's challenges began even earlier, with a phone call on January 7 that shattered everything.

It was Logan. His voice, usually steady despite his struggles, was shaking, panicked, and filled with terror. He was screaming, "She's gone, she's gone!" over and over, his words tumbling out so quickly that I could barely understand him. Finally, he managed to say, "Mom is gone. Mom is gone." It hit me like a freight train.

Gina, Logan's mother, had been found deceased in her apartment in Chicago. The cause appeared to be a heart attack. Logan was beside himself, panicked, frightened, and completely at a loss for what to do next. He called me not just because I was his father, but because in that moment, he needed someone to anchor him, to help him navigate the unthinkable.

I was floored. Gina had been a central figure in Logan's life and, by extension, mine. While our marriage had ended long ago, our connection as parents and co-guardians of Logan had endured. She had always been there for him, and now, suddenly, she was gone.

Logan was in Sarasota, Florida, completely alone. Gina's death left him not just grieving but untethered. He didn't know whether he should go to Chicago or what steps he needed to take.

His anguish over her death was compounded by the sheer logistical overwhelming pressure of handling her final arrangements.

For me, the grief was layered. I mourned for Logan, for the loss of Gina, and for the stark reality that my son, already struggling with so much, now faced this monumental loss. It was a pain I couldn't shield him from, and that broke my heart.

In the hours that followed, I reached out to Gina's sister Tammy and other family members. Together, we decided on the next steps. Gina would be cremated, and her ashes would be sent to Sarasota for a memorial service at the same funeral home where both of her parents had been remembered. It felt fitting, a way to honor her life and connect her passing to the family she loved so deeply.

Logan, lost in his grief, needed me. I didn't think twice. I hugged Randy goodbye, got in my car, and began the long drive from Little Rock to Sarasota. The miles stretched endlessly before me, giving me too much time to think, to worry, to grieve. I wanted to be there for Logan as quickly as possible, to help him carry the weight of this unimaginable loss.

The days that followed were a blur of planning, grieving, and trying to support Logan in any way I could. For him, Gina's death was a devastating blow, another profound loss added to a life already marked by hardship. It was a reminder of how fragile everything is, and how quickly the people we love can be taken from us.

Gina had been a wonderful mother, a loving sister, and a kind friend to many. Her death left a void not just for Logan but for everyone who knew her. And yet, in the midst of our grief, there was an unspoken understanding: we would honor her memory by supporting one another, by being there for Logan, and by ensuring that she was remembered with love.

The memorial service for Gina was a bittersweet reunion, bringing together family and friends who hadn't been in the same room for years. Her sister and her adult children flew in from up north, and Gina's lifelong best friend made the trip to deliver a heartfelt eulogy. My dad drove up from South Florida, determined to be there for Logan and to pay his respects. It was a testament to how loved Gina was, even by those she hadn't seen in a long time.

In true Gina fashion, though, the service didn't begin without a little drama. The schedule was set, and the attendees were gathered, but we were still waiting for Gina's remains to arrive.

Her remains were scheduled to be delivered to her brother's house, and as the start time approached, they were nowhere to be found. I couldn't help but find the humor in it, Gina was about to be late for her own funeral. Finally, at the last moment, her brothers arrived with Gina's remains, and we were able to begin.

Logan stood surrounded by family and friends, his grief raw and visible. The shock of losing his mother so suddenly was written all over him. Though he had faced loss before, this was different. Gina was his rock, the person who had been there through everything. Watching him navigate this moment of profound sorrow was one of the hardest things I've ever experienced as a parent. I wanted to protect him, to somehow make it easier, but all I could do was be there beside him.

The service itself was a beautiful tribute to Gina's life. Her best friend's eulogy painted a picture of her warmth, humor, and kindness, reminding everyone of the light she brought into their lives. It was clear how much she had been loved and how deeply she would be missed.

After the service, we gathered briefly to share stories and console one another. Then, as a family, we opened the box containing Gina's ashes. It was a surreal moment, one filled with both sadness and a sense of purpose. We carefully scooped out a small portion of her ashes and made our way to the cemetery where her parents were buried. Sprinkling her ashes there felt like bringing her home, reconnecting her with the people who had shaped her life and whom she loved so dearly. It was a quiet, sacred act, one that brought a measure of peace amidst the grief.

When the ceremony was over, I made a suggestion: we should all go to Yoder's for supper. The idea brought a flicker of lightness to the somber day. Yoder's, a beloved Amish restaurant in Sarasota, held special meaning for Gina and me. We ate there together even before Logan was born, and it had become a staple of our visits to Sarasota over the years. It felt fitting to gather there, to share a meal in her honor, and to let the comfort of tradition help soothe the ache of loss.

That evening, surrounded by family and the warm, welcoming atmosphere of Yoder's, we found a small measure of solace. The simple act of breaking bread together reminded us of the connections that remained, even in the face of such a profound loss. It was a moment of togetherness that Gina would have loved, a reminder that even in grief, there is love, laughter, and the enduring strength of family.

Chapter 36: A Moment of Clarity

During my time in Sarasota for Gina's memorial, something unexpected emerged from the sorrow of her passing: clarity about the extent to which Logan's addiction was influencing his relationships. While speaking with Tammy, Gina's sister, it became clear that Logan's struggles with addiction had created a web of manipulation and secrecy that affected all of us.

Tammy shared stories of Logan's calls to her, filled with desperate pleas for help. He had told her he needed money for food, transportation to work, and other seemingly urgent needs. They were the same kinds of stories he had told me. But in talking with Tammy, I learned he had also painted a very different picture of me and my family to Gina's side of the family. Logan had portrayed us as unhelpful, unloving, even cruel, "monsters," essentially. It was a gut punch to hear, but it wasn't entirely unexpected. Addiction thrives on isolation, and Logan had been working hard to keep all his worlds, me and my family, Gina's family, his friends, and coworkers, separate.

When Tammy and I realized we were both being manipulated by the same patterns, we decided enough was enough. Instead of letting addiction continue to divide us, we agreed to present a united front. This wasn't about anger or retribution, it was about recognizing that we couldn't let Logan's addiction play us against each other. We loved him, and we wanted to help him in ways that truly mattered, not in ways that would inadvertently enable his destructive behaviors.

The conversation with Tammy brought an unexpected sense of connection and relief. For years, Gina's family and I had been somewhat distant, but this shared experience reminded me of how much we all cared for Logan and wanted the best for him. One of Logan's cousins even remarked that I wasn't the "mean asshole" Logan had made me out to be. It was a bittersweet moment, knowing Logan had spun such narratives about me, but it also reaffirmed my belief in the need for honesty and transparency moving forward.

Logan's behavior was, unfortunately, indicative of how addiction controls and distorts relationships. Someone suffering with SUD often isolate their sources of support, telling one group one story and another group something entirely different. It's a way to maximize help and minimize accountability. For Logan, keeping Gina's family and mine in separate lanes allowed him to preserve his narrative and avoid facing the full picture of his addiction.

This kind of manipulation isn't born out of malice; it's a survival mechanism driven by the desperation and shame that come with addiction. Logan wasn't trying to hurt us; he was trying to navigate a life controlled by substances, and the addiction used his charm and resourcefulness to maintain its grip on him.

One unexpected blessing from this difficult period was reconnecting with Gina's family. Tammy and I talked more openly than we had in years, sharing not just stories of Logan but also memories of Gina and the life we had all shared. Other members of Gina's family began reaching out, and I found myself reconnecting with them on Facebook, where we could exchange updates, offer support, and keep the lines of communication open.

For too long, addiction had created barriers between us, but now we had the opportunity to rebuild those bridges. It felt like a small victory in the larger battle, a reminder that love and unity could still thrive, even in the face of loss and hardship.

As Gina's family and I worked together to navigate Logan's struggles, I felt a renewed sense of purpose. Logan's addiction had driven a wedge between us for years, but now we were united in our approach. By sharing information and presenting a consistent front, we hoped to help Logan see that his addiction couldn't divide us anymore.

This wasn't the end of Logan's challenges, but it was a turning point for us as a family. We had been played by his addiction, yes, but we refused to let it continue. In honoring Gina's memory and working together to support Logan, we found strength in our shared love for him, and for each other.

Chapter 37: The Life Insurance Dilemma

After Gina's passing, one of the many logistical and emotional challenges we faced was handling the life insurance policy tied to her job in the Chicago area. It wasn't a large policy, just $10,000, but to Logan, it seemed like a windfall. As the sole beneficiary, Logan signed the necessary paperwork to allow the funeral home to take its portion directly from the policy, covering Gina's final arrangements. This left over eight thousand dollars remaining, and Logan was desperate to get his hands on it.

Tammy and I both knew this was a dangerous situation. Given Logan's struggles with addiction, having access to such a significant sum of money was almost guaranteed to lead to trouble. We feared that instead of using the funds to stabilize his life, paying bills, securing housing, or covering everyday expenses, he would use it to feed his addiction. The consequences of that could be catastrophic.

In an effort to protect Logan, Tammy and I contacted the insurance company. Our hope was to have the remaining funds sent to a trust I managed on Logan's behalf. This way, the money could be used responsibly, ensuring it wouldn't contribute to his addiction. It seemed like a reasonable solution, one rooted in love and concern for Logan's well-being.

But the insurance company wouldn't hear of it. Their position was clear: unless Tammy or I were Logan's legal guardians, a status we didn't hold, we had no authority to redirect the funds. Logan was an adult, and as far as the insurance company was concerned, he had the sole right to decide how to use the money. No exceptions.

It was a devastating blow. We could see the danger so clearly, but the system left us powerless to intervene. It was yet another example of how addiction complicates every aspect of life, turning even something as straightforward as a life insurance payout into a potential crisis.

This experience underscored one of the most challenging aspects of parenting, or supporting, an adult with substance use disorder: the loss of control. Logan's addiction was a constant presence in his life, influencing his decisions and priorities in ways that were often harmful. As his father, I wanted to shield him from those consequences, to help him make better choices. But the reality of addiction, coupled with his legal autonomy, meant that I couldn't always protect him.

The insurance company's refusal to redirect the funds felt like a failure, even though I knew it wasn't my fault. It was a stark reminder of how addiction forces families to navigate a system that often doesn't account for the complexities of substance use disorder. Logan's legal rights as an adult clashed with the very real danger his addiction posed, leaving Tammy and me in a heartbreaking position.

Tammy and I had been working together to present a united front in supporting Logan without enabling his addiction. This situation tested that resolve. We had to accept that Logan would have access to the money, no matter how much we feared the outcome. The best we could do was offer guidance and hope that, somehow, he would make choices that wouldn't put him in harm's way.

It's a difficult thing to balance, loving someone unconditionally while also setting boundaries to protect them and yourself. Addiction doesn't just harm the person using; it ripples outward, affecting everyone who loves them. For Tammy and me, this was another painful chapter in a long story of trying to support Logan while navigating the limitations placed on us by his addiction and the systems that failed to provide real solutions.

In the end, Logan received the money in late April, 2020. What he did with it, I'll never fully know. Addiction often creates a fog of half-truths and unanswered questions, and this situation was no different. What I do know is that Tammy and I tried to do what was best for Logan, even when the system and the disease itself made it feel impossible. And in moments like these, the only thing left to hold onto was the hope that, despite the odds, Logan would find his way.

As we later found out, Logan had taken matters into his own hands. Despite having initially signed paperwork allowing the funeral home to deduct its costs from Gina's life insurance policy, he contacted the insurance company on his own and revoked the arrangement. Instead, he demanded that the entire $10,000 be sent directly to him.

This revelation was devastating but, sadly, not surprising. Logan's addiction often drove him to make impulsive decisions, and the lure of having the full sum in his hands, no doubt influenced by the addiction's grip, was too much for him to resist. It wasn't about disrespecting his mother's memory; it was about the desperate pull of the disease controlling his life.

The process of changing the payout arrangement took several months, and it wasn't until April 2020 that Logan finally received the full $10,000. By that time, the world was deep into the chaos of the COVID-19 pandemic, adding another layer of complexity and isolation to an already fragile situation.

Having access to the entire sum of $10,000 was not the blessing it might have seemed on the surface. For someone battling addiction, sudden access to a large amount of money is often more of a curse. It represents not just opportunity but temptation, and the potential consequences can be devastating.

For Logan, this money became a pivotal moment. While I don't know every detail of how he spent it, the reality of addiction makes it easy to guess. Whether it went toward substances, debts, or fleeting comforts, it was clear that the money didn't bring him stability or healing. Instead, it likely deepened the challenges he was already facing.

This chapter in Logan's life underscored several painful truths about addiction:

The pull of immediate gratification is strong in those suffering from SUD. Addiction thrives on urgency and impulsivity. Logan's decision to revoke the funeral home's payment arrangement wasn't born out of logic or malice, it was a reaction to the overwhelming need to control the funds and use them in ways that felt urgent to him at the moment.

By going directly to the insurance company, Logan bypassed the family members trying to support him. Addiction often isolates people, driving a wedge between them and those who love them. It's a cruel irony that the very support network someone suffering with SUD need most is often the one they push away.

This situation also highlighted the systemic challenges families face when trying to help someone with addiction. Despite our best efforts to protect Logan from himself, the legal system and the insurance company's policies left us powerless to intervene. It was another reminder that loving someone with substance use disorder means constantly bumping up against the limits of what you can control.

As Logan's father, watching this unfold was one of the hardest parts of my journey with him. I wanted so desperately to shield him from the consequences of his addiction, to help him find a path to healing. But the reality was, I couldn't make his decisions for him. I had to stand by, heart in hand, as he navigated this on his own. It was a painful reminder that love, no matter how deep, can't always fix what's broken.

In the time that followed, the fallout from this decision became clear. Logan was still struggling, still caught in the cycle of addiction. The money he fought so hard to get didn't save him; it simply gave his addiction more fuel. And yet, even in the midst of my heartbreak, I held onto hope. I believed in the Logan I knew, the kind, compassionate, and charming person who was still there, fighting to break free.

Chapter 38: The Struggle to Surrender

When Logan and I discussed how he should use the money from Gina's life insurance, I emphasized the importance of being responsible. I reminded him of the $1,700 he owed the funeral home for his mother's memorial and urged him to take care of it. He assured me he would, and I wanted so badly to believe him. But in the same breath, Logan admitted he had started using heroin again. My heart sank.

It wasn't the first time we had this kind of conversation, but this time felt heavier. He told me he wanted to stop, and that gave me hope. We began exploring options for rehab, and I brought up a program in Arkansas that had an excellent reputation. It was a one-year, cost-effective, faith-based program. I had connections through friends whose sister had completed the program, and they vouched for its success rate. Even better, the director worked with Logan, Sarasota law enforcement, and the judicial system to arrange for Logan to enter the program without facing additional legal consequences. Everything seemed aligned for him to take this step toward recovery.

But just days before Logan was scheduled to fly to Arkansas, he told me he wasn't coming. His reason? The program was faith-based. He couldn't see himself committing to it because it required participants to embrace the concept of a higher power.

Logan's hesitation highlighted a fundamental aspect of addiction: the illusion of control. Addiction thrives on the idea that the person using substances is in charge, even as their life spirals further out of control. For Logan, the idea of surrendering to a higher power likely felt like an admission of defeat. He may have thought, I can fix this myself. I don't need faith or anyone else to help me. This mindset isn't uncommon among someone suffering with SUD.

Substance use disorder fundamentally alters thought patterns, reinforcing feelings of self-reliance and denial. The brain becomes wired to seek instant gratification and avoid anything that challenges the addiction's dominance. Admitting that help is needed, especially in a faith-based context, can feel like losing the last shred of autonomy they believe they have.

Faith-based recovery programs often require participants to confront their vulnerabilities and acknowledge that they can't overcome addiction alone. This surrender isn't just about religion; it's about recognizing that the addiction is bigger than they are and that healing requires external support, whether from God, a higher power, or a community of people invested in their recovery.

Logan's resistance to this idea may have stemmed from a combination of fear, pride, and the grip of his addiction. Acknowledging a higher power or accepting the need for faith based help might have felt like admitting that he wasn't in control, a terrifying prospect for someone already battling the chaos of addiction. For many suffering with SUD, the idea of surrendering control, even to something benevolent, feels like giving up.

Addiction not only affects a person's physical health but also rewires their cognitive and emotional processes. Logan's reluctance to attend the faith-based program reflected how addiction distorts thinking:

Faith-based programs often involve structured routines, regular accountability, and introspection, elements that can feel overwhelming to someone used to the unstructured chaos of addiction. The thought of facing his own actions and choices in such a transparent way may have been intimidating for Logan.

Recovery requires change, and change is inherently uncomfortable. Faith-based programs often challenge participants to reevaluate their values, beliefs, and coping mechanisms. Logan may have been afraid of stepping into the unknown, especially when addiction provided him with a warped sense of stability.

Addiction fosters a false sense of independence, I can quit whenever I want; I just don't want to right now. Accepting help, particularly from a program rooted in faith, meant admitting he couldn't do it on his own. That level of vulnerability was likely deeply unsettling for him.

When Logan told me he wasn't coming to Arkansas, I was heartbroken. I had seen a glimmer of hope, a path forward, and it felt like it had been snatched away. But at the same time, I understood. Addiction is a battle of wills, not just against the substance but against oneself. Logan wasn't ready to take that step, and I couldn't force him. Successful recovery has to be chosen, not imposed, and that's one of the hardest truths for a parent to accept.

I wanted to believe that Logan's admission that he had been using again was a step toward honesty and accountability. And maybe it was. But the pull of addiction, combined with his resistance to surrender, ultimately kept him from taking the next step.

Logan's rejection of the program didn't diminish my belief in his ability to recover. I knew that his hesitation wasn't about faith itself, it was about the fear of losing control and confronting the depth of his struggles. Faith-based or not, I believed that recovery was possible for him, even if it had to happen on his own timeline.

As a parent, it's devastating to watch your child turn away from help, but it's also a reminder of the complexity of addiction. It's not just about willpower or making the right choice; it's about battling an internal force that reshapes every thought, every action, and every decision. The drug of choice was merely his method of quieting the noise in his head and provided some relief from the pressures of what underlying issues were tormenting him.

Chapter 39: The Need to Treat Underlying Issues

Addiction is rarely just about the substance itself. It's a coping mechanism, a way to numb emotional pain, escape mental anguish, or fill a void caused by trauma, unmet needs, or unresolved psychological struggles. For true recovery to happen, it's not enough to address the addiction on the surface level; the deeper issues fueling the addiction must also be confronted and treated. Unfortunately, many recovery programs focus primarily on detox and abstinence, leaving the root causes of the addiction unexamined and unresolved.

Addiction often stems from unhealed wounds, whether those are from childhood trauma, mental health challenges, or other painful experiences. For many suffering with SUD, substances provide a temporary escape from these feelings, dulling their pain and silencing the thoughts that torment them. Logan once described to me how his addiction felt like a way to stop his brain from racing, a way to quiet the overwhelming noise in his head. That insight was heartbreaking because it showed me that he wasn't just fighting a physical dependency, he was fighting to escape his own mind.

Hindsight has given me more clarity about Logan's struggles. As a parent, you do your best to provide love, support, and stability, but you don't always see the full picture. The traumas that shape a child's inner world are often hidden, only revealing themselves through their actions years later. Logan's battles with addiction weren't just about a substance; they were about trying to cope with feelings and experiences he couldn't otherwise process.

Addiction is a symptom of deeper pain. If the underlying issues aren't addressed, the addict is left with the same mental and emotional struggles that led them to use substances in the first place. Without tools to process and heal from these struggles, the cycle of numbing and avoidance is likely to continue, even after periods of sobriety.

Trauma can be a significant driver of relapse. When a person is triggered by unresolved memories, emotions, or circumstances, their brain often defaults to the coping mechanisms it knows best, substances. Treating trauma can reduce the likelihood of relapse by helping individuals build healthier ways to manage their emotional pain.

Recovery isn't just about stopping the use of substances; it's about rebuilding a life. To do that, those suffering with SUD need to understand what led them down the path of addiction in the first place. By addressing the trauma and underlying issues, they can begin to redefine themselves in a way that isn't centered on pain or avoidance.

As we discussed previously, many recovery programs fail to adequately address the mental and emotional pain behind addiction. Detox programs often focus on immediate physical withdrawal, and even longer-term rehabs may prioritize sobriety milestones over holistic healing. Therapy or counseling is sometimes included, but it's often surface-level and doesn't go deep enough to confront the root causes.

Faith-based programs, while valuable for some, can also fall short when participants resist or struggle with the spiritual component. Logan's hesitation to enter a faith-based program, for instance, wasn't just about religion, it was about his reluctance to surrender to something bigger than himself, to face the vulnerability required for true healing. For many suffering from SUD, this kind of deep introspection is the scariest part of recovery.

As a parent, I've often found myself reflecting on Logan's life, wondering what I missed and what I could have done differently. At the moment, it's easy to focus on the immediate challenges, school performance, behavioral issues, or moments of rebellion, without seeing the underlying pain driving those behaviors. It's only in hindsight that the patterns become clearer.

I believe that Logan's addiction was his way of coping with mental pain he couldn't express. He struggled with self-worth, anxiety, and a sense of chaos that he tried to quiet with substances. At the time, I didn't fully grasp the depth of his struggles. I saw the symptoms, his defiance, his choices, his addiction, but not the trauma underneath. It's a lesson I've had to learn the hard way: addiction doesn't arise in a vacuum, and healing requires more than just stopping the behavior. It requires understanding and addressing the pain that caused it.

For recovery to be truly effective, it needs to be holistic. This means addressing not only the addiction but also the person's mental, emotional, and even spiritual well-being. It's about teaching coping mechanisms, fostering self-awareness, and helping those with SUD rebuild their sense of self-worth.

Programs should include evidence-based therapies like cognitive-behavioral therapy (CBT), dialectical behavior therapy (DBT), or trauma-focused approaches that help individuals process their pain in a safe, supportive environment.

Many suffering with SUD struggle with co-occurring mental health disorders, such as depression or anxiety. Treating these alongside the addiction is essential for long-term recovery.

Isolation feeds addiction, while connection fosters healing. Recovery programs should emphasize building healthy relationships and support networks to replace the void that substances once filled.

Logan's journey has taught me that addiction is deeply tied to how a person perceives their life. For him, substances were a way to numb the pain of feeling like he wasn't enough or that his life was too overwhelming to face. Recognizing this has helped me understand him more deeply, not just as someone who struggled with addiction but as someone who was doing his best to survive in the only way he knew how.

As parents and loved ones, it's our job to see past the addiction and into the heart of the person we care for. To ask not just; Why won't they stop? But What are they running from? And How can I help them face it? It's not an easy road, but it's the one that leads to true healing.

Chapter 40: A Lifeline in Logan's Struggle

Despite everything Logan was going through, our daily phone calls remained a constant in both of our lives. No matter how far apart we were geographically, those conversations kept us connected. For me, they were a way to check in, to remind him that I loved him and was there for him, even as I worried about the toll addiction was taking on him. For Logan, I hope they provided a sense of stability and a reminder that he wasn't alone, even when the world felt overwhelming.

It was clear in those calls that Logan was struggling. His voice often carried the weight of his battles, even when he tried to sound upbeat. He talked about his frustrations, his attempts to stay clean, and the things that gave him fleeting moments of hope. But underneath it all was the unmistakable tension of someone grappling with addiction, a tension I couldn't fix, no matter how much I wanted to.

Logan's aunt Tammy was also a critical part of his support system during this time. Like me, she could see that he was struggling and did her best to offer love and encouragement from a distance. Together, we tried to surround Logan with as much care as we could, even if the miles between us made it hard to intervene directly.

We often compared notes, sharing what we'd learned from our conversations with him and trying to piece together the full picture of his life. Addiction thrives on secrecy, and Logan, like

167

many suffering with SUD, had a way of telling different stories to different people. By staying in close communication, Tammy and I hoped to bridge the gaps and create a united front, one that Logan couldn't easily divide.

Supporting Logan from afar was one of the most challenging aspects of this time. Addiction is a deeply isolating disease, and while I knew Logan needed love and connection, I also knew that I couldn't physically be there to provide it. The daily phone calls helped, but they often left me feeling helpless. I could listen, offer advice, and express my love, but I couldn't pull him out of the darkness he was in.

Tammy and I shared this frustration. We both wanted to do more, to be there for Logan in a tangible way, but we were limited by the realities of distance and the boundaries we had to maintain to protect ourselves from being drawn too far into his addiction.

Despite the challenges, those daily calls were a testament to the strength of our bond. Logan knew he could always pick up the phone and talk to me, no matter what. Even when he was at his lowest, he didn't shut me out entirely. That gave me hope, hope that somewhere deep inside, he knew he was loved, and that love might eventually help him find his way to recovery.

For me, those conversations were bittersweet. They were a reminder of the son I loved, the witty, compassionate, and charismatic Logan who could make me laugh even in the darkest moments. But they were also a reminder of how much he was hurting, how much he was fighting against something bigger than himself.

Together, Tammy and I did our best to support Logan from a distance. We couldn't walk his path for him, but we could let him know we were there, cheering him on and ready to help him take the next step when he was ready. It wasn't perfect, and it wasn't enough to save him from his struggles, but it was what we could do.

Looking back, I hold onto those phone calls as precious memories. They were proof that, no matter how far addiction tried to pull Logan away, he was still reaching out, still trying to stay connected. And as his father, that connection meant everything to me.

Chapter 41: Logan and Narcan

One of the most unsettling conversations I had with Logan during this time came when he openly shared that Narcan had been administered to him after he overdosed on heroin laced with fentanyl. Hearing him casually discuss such a life threatening event was difficult enough, but his response to my concern left me stunned. When I asked if it was worth continuing to use heroin when he didn't know if it was laced with fentanyl, he told me, "It's OK because Narcan is available, and somebody will always be around to administer it."

Logan's belief that Narcan was a safety net against the dangers of heroin use was alarming. It reflected not only the dangerous rationalizations that addiction fosters but also a misunderstanding of what Narcan is truly meant for. When I pressed further, asking what he planned to do about the fentanyl crisis, his response was equally shocking: he said he would ask his heroin dealer to make sure there was no fentanyl in his supply. It was a heartbreaking moment, realizing that Logan wasn't ready to take the step I was hoping for, the one where he would say, I want to get clean. I don't want to die. Instead, his thinking was still shaped by addiction's grip, focused on managing risk rather than escaping it.

Narcan, the brand name for naloxone, is a medication designed to reverse the effects of an opioid overdose. It works by binding to the opioid receptors in the brain, effectively blocking the effects of substances like heroin, fentanyl, and opioid based prescription painkillers. When administered during an overdose,

Narcan can restore normal breathing and prevent death in a matter of minutes.

Narcan is typically available as a nasal spray or an injectable solution, and it has become a vital tool in combating the opioid epidemic. First responders, medical professionals, and even bystanders can use it to save lives. It's widely distributed in many communities, often given to people at high risk of overdose or their loved ones.

While Narcan is undeniably lifesaving, it is not a cure for addiction, nor is it a "safety net" that makes opioid use safe. Logan's belief that he could rely on Narcan as a fallback reflected a dangerous misunderstanding of its role.

Narcan can save a person's life in the event of an overdose, but it does nothing to address the underlying addiction. Without comprehensive treatment and support, many people saved by Narcan will return to using, perpetuating the cycle of addiction and overdose.

Fentanyl, a synthetic opioid that is 50-100 times stronger than morphine, has become a deadly contaminant in the illicit drug supply. Even a tiny amount can cause a fatal overdose, and the presence of fentanyl in drugs like heroin, cocaine, and counterfeit pills is often unknown to users. Narcan's ability to reverse a fentanyl overdose is limited by how much of the drug is in a person's system; in some cases, multiple doses of Narcan are required, and even then, it may not be enough.

Like Logan, some people develop a false sense of security around Narcan, believing that its availability makes opioid use less risky. This mindset can lead to riskier behaviors, such as using alone or taking higher doses, under the assumption that someone will always be there to administer Narcan if something goes wrong. Unfortunately, this isn't always the case.

Narcan is a critical tool in saving lives, but it should never be seen as a justification for continued opioid use. It's important to understand the limitations of Narcan.

While Narcan can reverse an overdose, it does nothing to mitigate other risks of opioid use, such as infections from needle sharing, legal consequences, or the physical and emotional toll of addiction.

Addiction is a chronic disease that requires treatment and support. Narcan can interrupt a fatal overdose, but without follow-up care, the person is likely to return to using. Comprehensive treatment programs that address the root causes of addiction, such as trauma or mental health issues, are essential for long-term recovery.

Fentanyl's potency and prevalence in the drug supply make opioid use more dangerous than ever. Even seasoned users who think they "know their limits" are at risk of overdosing because of fentanyl contamination.

Logan's responses during this conversation were deeply rooted in the mindset of addiction. Addiction changes the way a person thinks, prioritizing the need for the substance over logic, safety, or long-term goals. His belief that Narcan made heroin use acceptable and that his dealer could guarantee a fentanyl free supply reflected the distorted reasoning that addiction fosters.

Logan's reliance on Narcan showed how addiction can lead to a denial of the true risks involved. He was focused on surviving each moment rather than addressing the larger picture of his addiction and the dangers it posed.

Addiction often makes people feel powerless, leading them to put their trust in external factors like dealers or Narcan instead of taking steps toward recovery. Logan's response about asking his dealer to avoid fentanyl highlighted this lack of agency, a tragic reality for many battling addictions.

Recovery requires facing the pain and trauma that addiction has numbed. For Logan, the idea of getting clean and stepping into a program likely felt overwhelming and terrifying. His rationalizations about Narcan and his dealer may have been a way to avoid confronting the deeper work of recovery.

As his father, this conversation left me reeling. I wanted so desperately for Logan to say, I want help. I don't want to die. Instead, I heard the rationalizations of a young man still in the grip of addiction, trying to make sense of his world through the lens of the disease controlling him. It broke my heart, but it also deepened my resolve to keep supporting him in any way I could.

Narcan (naloxone) is an opioid antagonist, meaning it blocks the effects of opioids on the brain. When someone is experiencing an opioid overdose, Narcan can rapidly reverse the life-threatening symptoms, particularly respiratory depression, which is the primary cause of death in overdoses. Here's what happens when Narcan is administered and how the overdose victim typically responds:

Blocking Opioid Receptors: Narcan works by binding to the same receptors in the brain that opioids target. These are known as opioid receptors, which control pain relief, euphoria, and, critically, breathing. When opioids like heroin, fentanyl, or prescription painkillers overwhelm these receptors, they slow or stop breathing. Narcan displaces the opioids from the receptors, effectively blocking their effects and allowing the person to breathe again.

Within 1-3 minutes of administration, Narcan typically begins to work. It restores normal breathing and increases oxygen levels in the brain, preventing further damage or death. In some cases, more than one dose may be required, especially with potent opioids like fentanyl.

When Narcan takes effect, the response can be dramatic. Many individuals who were unresponsive or near death may regain consciousness quickly. This can be a jarring experience, as they were likely unaware of the overdose and may feel disoriented. Narcan can precipitate acute opioid withdrawal, especially in those who are physically dependent. Common withdrawal symptoms include:

- Agitation or irritability
- Nausea or vomiting
- Sweating or chills
- Muscle aches
- Anxiety or restlessness
- Diarrhea

These symptoms occur because Narcan not only blocks the overdose but also abruptly removes the euphoric and pain relieving effects of opioids. The victim's body goes from being flooded with opioids to having none of their effects in a matter of minutes, which can feel physically and emotionally distressing.

Overdose victims may not immediately understand what happened. The sudden shift in their state, combined with the onset of withdrawal, can lead to feelings of anger or fear. Some may become combative or resistant, especially if they were unaware they overdosed.

Narcan's effects typically last between 30 to 90 minutes. Because it temporarily blocks opioids, there's a risk of re-overdose if the person has high levels of opioids in their system or takes more opioids after regaining consciousness. This is why medical attention is critical even after Narcan is administered.

Emergency responders or bystanders administering Narcan should call 911 immediately. Even if the person appears stable, ongoing medical evaluation is necessary. In some cases, Narcan may wear off before the opioids are fully metabolized, causing the overdose symptoms to return.

Narcan is a lifesaving intervention, but it's not a cure for addiction. It addresses the immediate crisis of an overdose, giving the individual a second chance at life. However, the trauma of an overdose, combined with the abrupt withdrawal symptoms Narcan induces, can leave the individual shaken, confused, and in need of compassionate follow-up care.

When Logan told me Narcan had been used on him, I tried to imagine what that moment must have been like. I pictured him lying unconscious, his breathing slowed or stopped, and someone stepping in with the nasal spray or injection that brought him back to life. It was a relief to know he had been saved, but it was also devastating to realize how close he had come to not surviving. The fact that Narcan had become part of his life, a tool he assumed would always be there, was a stark reminder of the dangerous path he was on.

Narcan gave Logan another chance, but it didn't solve the deeper issues that led to his overdose. Those issues required more than medication, they required compassion, understanding, and a willingness on his part to seek help. And that's the hardest part of addiction: Narcan can bring someone back from the brink of death, but the journey to recovery is one they must choose for themselves.

Chapter 42: The Broader Societal Implications of Narcan

Narcan (naloxone) has become a cornerstone in the fight against the opioid epidemic. Its ability to reverse opioid overdoses within minutes has saved countless lives, making it an essential tool in harm reduction strategies. However, its widespread use has sparked debates about its implications for public health, addiction treatment, and societal attitudes toward substance use. Below is an exploration of the societal impact of Narcan, both positive and challenging.

Narcan has saved thousands of lives by reversing potentially fatal overdoses. According to the CDC, there were over 100,000 drug overdose deaths in the U.S. in a 12-month period ending in April 2021, with opioids involved in nearly 75% of those deaths. Narcan is often the difference between life and death in these situations, giving individuals a chance to seek recovery.

Programs that distribute Narcan to first responders, healthcare providers, and community members, including friends and family of those at risk, have empowered everyday people to act in emergencies. This has created a broader safety net in communities hard-hit by the opioid epidemic.

The availability of Narcan has helped shift some conversations about addiction from moral judgment to public health. By treating overdose as a medical emergency rather than a personal failing, Narcan reinforces the idea that people struggling with addiction deserve care and compassion.

While Narcan is a vital tool, its use raises complex societal questions and challenges.

Critics argue that Narcan may unintentionally create a false sense of security among opioid users, encouraging riskier behaviors under the assumption that Narcan will always be available to save them. This mindset, while not universally true, has been echoed in statements like Logan's belief that Narcan was a safeguard against fentanyl-laced heroin.

Some individuals are revived with Narcan multiple times, raising concerns about its long-term effectiveness in reducing overall opioid use. Critics worry that Narcan treats the symptoms (overdose) but not the root causes of addiction, perpetuating a cycle of survival without addressing recovery.

While Narcan is increasingly available, cost and distribution disparities remain. Community organizations and governments often struggle to ensure widespread access, particularly in rural or underserved areas. Critics argue that the focus on Narcan availability must be paired with investments in addiction treatment and prevention to create lasting change.

One of the most significant opportunities presented by Narcan is its potential to act as a gateway to addiction treatment. Surviving an overdose can be a wake-up call for some individuals, prompting them to seek help. Programs that pair Narcan distribution with resources for addiction treatment and recovery support can help capitalize on this critical moment.

Emergency rooms and first responders are increasingly incorporating Narcan into broader strategies for addressing addiction. For example, some hospitals now provide immediate referrals to addiction specialists or start medication-assisted treatment (MAT) for individuals revived with Narcan.

While Narcan is an essential harm-reduction tool, it doesn't address the root causes of addiction. Broader societal changes are necessary to complement its use.

Communities need more access to comprehensive addiction treatment programs, mental health services, and support networks. Narcan saves lives in the moment, but recovery requires long-term care.

Treating addiction as a medical condition rather than a criminal act can reduce the stigma that prevents people from seeking help. Policies that prioritize harm reduction and rehabilitation over punishment align with Narcan's lifesaving mission.

Educating the public about Narcan's purpose and limitations is crucial. People need to understand that while Narcan can reverse an overdose, it's not a solution to addiction or a justification for risky behavior.

Narcan's widespread use has forced society to confront the reality of the opioid epidemic. It has challenged outdated views of addiction as a moral failing and emphasized the importance of compassion and care. However, changing societal attitudes takes time and requires ongoing effort.

Every life saved by Narcan is a reminder that people with substance use disorders are not disposable. These moments challenge the stigma surrounding addiction and reinforce the need for empathetic responses.

The success of Narcan highlights the importance of harm reduction strategies, approaches that aim to minimize the negative consequences of drug use rather than eliminate it entirely. This shift represents a more pragmatic and compassionate approach to addressing addiction.

Narcan is a lifesaving tool, but it's not a standalone solution to the opioid epidemic. Its role must be part of a broader strategy that includes expanded access to recovery services. Saving someone from an overdose is only the first step. Communities need robust recovery programs to support individuals after they're revived.

The rise of fentanyl and its analogs has made Narcan more critical than ever. Policies addressing the trafficking and contamination of drugs with fentanyl are essential to reducing overdose deaths; however they are not the only solution to this crisis.

Addiction impacts entire communities. Resources for families, harm reduction education, and community-based support systems are vital to creating a safer and healthier environment.

Narcan is one of the most powerful tools we have in the fight against the opioid epidemic, but it's not a solution in itself. It saves lives, giving people another chance, but it doesn't address the underlying trauma, mental health issues, or systemic inequalities that fuel addiction. To truly combat the opioid crisis, we must pair Narcan's lifesaving potential with comprehensive prevention, treatment, and recovery strategies that address addiction at its roots. Only then can we create lasting change.

Chapter 43: Camping Adventures

In the spring of 2020, amidst the chaos of the world and Logan's struggles, Randy and I found a welcome distraction in our shared love of camping. We had stumbled upon a 20-yearold travel trailer for under $4,000, a real find, and decided to give it a full makeover. It became our little project, transforming the camper into a cozy getaway that was as comfortable as it was functional.

We painted the interior, removed the old stove, oven, and anything else propane-related (we always did our cooking outside anyway), and installed a small electric fireplace that added a touch of charm. The fireplace was one of my favorite features, it made the camper feel like a tiny home on wheels. Logan used to tease me endlessly about our setup. He'd laugh and say, "You're not really camping. You're just outside." He wasn't wrong! But we embraced the idea of camping with creature comforts, and those lighthearted jokes from Logan made the whole experience even more fun.

By May 2020, we had a trip planned to Maumelle Campground, a beautiful spot right in Little Rock. It was going to be a special getaway because our dear friends, Steve and Laura, had just purchased their very first camper. They were as excited about their new adventure as we had been when we started. The plan was for Randy and me to check in on Wednesday, May 20th, with Steve and Laura joining us the next day, fresh from picking up their brand-new camper.

Camping wasn't just a retreat for Randy and me, it was something that brought joy to our little white schnauzer, Hanz, as well. He absolutely loved it. Hanz had a sixth sense of when we were preparing for a camping trip. The moment he saw the camper being loaded or gear being packed, his excitement was palpable. At the campground, he was always well-behaved, sticking close to us and enjoying the new sights and smells. Watching him trot around happily at our side made every trip that much more special.

That trip to Maumelle felt like a perfect slice of normalcy during a tumultuous year. While the world wrestled with the uncertainty of a global pandemic, and Logan's challenges loomed in my heart, camping offered a break from the stress. It was a chance to connect with friends, enjoy the outdoors, and find some peace in the simple pleasures of life.

Logan's jokes about our camping style often echoed in my mind during these trips, bringing a smile to my face. His humor was one of the many things I cherished about him, and even when we were miles apart, those little memories reminded me of the bond we shared.

When Randy and I moved to Little Rock in 2013, we started a non-medical home care agency. It was fulfilling work, primarily serving about 40 clients in an independent retirement community, many of whom had dementia. The relationships we built with those clients were deeply rewarding, but the work was also emotionally demanding. That's where camping came in and became our escape, our way to recharge and reconnect with nature and each other.

Camping wasn't just a getaway; it was a passion project. I was constantly searching online for ways to improve our little camper, always on the lookout for unique finds and upgrades that would make our trips more enjoyable. One day, while scrolling through marketplace listings, I stumbled upon a deal too good to pass up: an electric awning that would fit our camper. Normally, these awnings cost thousands of dollars, but this one was just $400. It felt like hitting the jackpot!

The awning became our next big project, and we were determined to have it installed and fully operational before our upcoming trip to Maumelle Campground. While the deal was incredible, the challenge of installing it was no small task. There's something about setting a goal like that, having a deadline, a clear purpose, and the excitement of seeing the finished result, that makes even hard work feel rewarding.

Randy and I dove into the project with the kind of determination that only comes from knowing how much joy the end result will bring. It wasn't just about having a fancy new feature on the camper; it was about enhancing the experience of sitting outside, rain or shine, and enjoying the beauty of the outdoors with friends, family, and our beloved schnauzer, Hanz, by our side.

With the awning project underway, our excitement for the upcoming trip grew even more. It wasn't just about the destination or the gear, it was about the time spent together, the laughs we knew we'd share with Steve and Laura, and the sense of freedom that only camping could provide. The anticipation of sitting under our new awning, watching the sun set over the Arkansas River, made all the effort worthwhile.

On a warm May day, Randy and I headed out early to our friend Ann's house in the country, where we kept our camper. The air was full of spring's promise, with the world coming alive again after winter's quiet. The excitement of a new camping project had us both eager to get started. While I had never installed an electric awning before, I had done my homework, watching online videos to get a handle on the steps involved. I've always loved tackling projects, but Randy? Not so much. Still, we were both committed to making this awning a reality.

The first step was removing the old awning, a task that turned out to be less daunting than I had anticipated. Once that was out of the way, we laid out all the parts for the new awning, taking a moment to double-check everything before moving forward. It wasn't just about getting it done; it was about doing it right.

Attaching the new awning to the camper was straightforward enough, at first. But as with any project, challenges arose. We needed to drill holes to run the wires for the awning's motor, and that meant sealing the new openings with silicone to ensure they were watertight. It was a bit more involved than I had planned, but step by step, we made steady progress.

With everything in place, it was finally time for the moment of truth: pressing the button to see if the awning would actually work. I could feel Randy's skepticism, he wasn't as confident about these projects as I was. But as I pressed the button, the awning sprang to life, extending smoothly and perfectly.

Much to Randy's surprise (and maybe mine, too), it worked like a charm! Seeing the awning in action was incredibly satisfying. All the effort, the problem-solving, and the teamwork had paid off. It was one of those moments where you can't help but step back, admire the result, and feel a little proud.

For Randy and me, this wasn't just about installing an awning. It was about working together to create something that would enhance our camping adventures. While Randy might not have been as enthusiastic about the process, his smile when the awning worked said it all. It was a reminder that even projects that seem tedious or daunting at first can become meaningful when shared.

Chapter 44: The Call That Changed Everything

It was around 2:00 in the afternoon, and Randy and I were standing outside the camper, watching the awning go in and out. We were celebrating the success of our hard work, laughing and enjoying the moment. Then my phone rang. It was my dad.

He asked me what I was doing, and I told him, still smiling, that we had just installed the awning, and it was working perfectly.

But then the tone of the conversation shifted. There was a heaviness in his voice as he said, "I need to talk to you about Logan."

I knew immediately. My heart sank. Before he could say more, I blurted out, "He's dead, isn't he?"

There was a pause. Then, with a somber tone I hadn't heard from him since my mother passed, my father responded, "Yes."

He explained that he had received a call from a detective in Sarasota. Logan had been found in his bed, the victim of an apparent overdose. My biggest fear, my worst nightmare, had just come true. My son, Logan, was gone.

I couldn't speak. I couldn't stand. I couldn't even breathe. Everything inside me collapsed. It felt as though the world had stopped spinning, leaving me trapped in a void of pain and disbelief. Somehow, I managed to ask my father to give me a few minutes to gather myself. He told me he loved me, and we hung up.

I sank to the ground right there next to the camper and let out a scream, a sound so raw and guttural that it startled Randy. He turned to me in shock, realizing instantly that something terrible had happened. Our friend Ann, hearing the commotion, came running outside to see what was going on. Randy, his voice trembling, told her, "He just got a call that Logan is dead."

Ann's face fell, her own memories of loss surfacing. She had lost a nephew to an overdose just a few years earlier and understood the magnitude of my pain. She knelt beside me, wrapping her arms around me as I sobbed, her presence was a small comfort in an otherwise unbearable moment.

The reality of Logan's death was incomprehensible. It was a moment I had feared for years, the outcome I had fought so hard to prevent, yet it had arrived all the same. The plans, the hopes, the constant effort to support him, all of it felt meaningless in the face of this loss. The son I loved so deeply, who had struggled so hard, was gone.

As I sat there, surrounded by Randy and Ann, my mind raced with questions, memories, and overwhelming traumatic grief. How had it come to this? Had he been alone in those final moments? Did he know how much he was loved?

I couldn't stop thinking about the last time we had spoken, about the moments we had shared, and about all the things I still wanted to say to him. The pain was suffocating, but it was nothing compared to the void his absence would leave in my life.

Chapter 45: The First Steps of My Grief

In the moments after receiving the news about Logan's death, my emotions were a hurricane, grief, shock, disbelief, and devastation all swirling together. It's hard to explain the depth of that pain. Everything felt like a blur, but somehow, I managed to pull myself together just enough to grab a notebook and pen. I sat at the table on Ann's porch, lit a cigarette, and called my father back.

My father was just as heartbroken as I was. The weight of making that call to me must have been unbearable for him. At least I heard the news from someone I knew and loved, someone who cared about me and understood the gravity of the moment. But for him, the call had come from a stranger, a detective in Sarasota delivering the unimaginable news that his grandson was gone. I can't even imagine how that must have felt for him.

During that call, my dad gave me the contact information for the detective in Sarasota. Knowing there were now endless tasks to manage, I hung up and steadied myself to make the call. Randy, always by my side, had already informed our friends Steve and Laura, as well as one of our employees, Molly, about what had happened. Their support was immediate and unwavering, even as I began to process the enormity of the loss.

When I called the detective, she calmly walked me through the details. Logan's roommate had called 911 around 1:00 PM Florida time, saying that Logan was unresponsive and appeared to be dead. She explained to the detective that earlier, at about noon, she had noticed Logan wasn't up yet. She cracked his bedroom door open so Logan's dog could come out and then took the dog outside.

When she returned, she decided to check on Logan again. That's when she found him in his bed, lying on his back, motionless. She told the detective that he looked peaceful. The thought of Logan being at peace brought me a sliver of comfort, but it was quickly drowned out by the storm of questions swirling in my mind.

The detective patiently answered as many of my questions as she could, but the answers only led to more questions. Had he been alone in his final moments? What had led to this overdose, was it fentanyl again? Had there been signs I missed in our recent conversations? Did he know how much he was loved, or did he feel alone?

Every detail she shared painted a clearer picture of Logan's last hours, but it also deepened the pain. Knowing that he had died in his bed, on his back, looking peaceful, offered some solace, it meant he hadn't suffered or struggled. But the knowledge that his life had ended this way was unbearable.

The detective explained the next steps, including the medical examiner's role and the process of handling Logan's remains. It was all so clinical and procedural, a stark contrast to the emotions tearing through me. But in the haze of grief, I knew I needed to focus. There were decisions to make, calls to return, and arrangements to be made. Yet all I wanted was to scream, cry, and somehow undo what had happened.

One detail that stuck with me was Logan's dog. His loyal companion had been there, likely sensing something was wrong but unable to do anything. I couldn't help but think about how much Logan had loved that dog and how much comfort the dog must have brought him, even in his final days. The image of his dog waiting by the door, watching his human with love and concern, broke my heart all over again.

As I sat on Ann's porch I tried to organize my thoughts and prepare for what lay ahead. There was so much to do, and yet I felt utterly paralyzed. The loss of Logan was a weight I couldn't yet fully grasp. My son was gone, and no amount of preparation or action could change that. But I knew I had to keep going, for Logan, for myself, and for the family and friends who would be devastated by this news.

Ann stayed close by, her presence a quiet comfort. Having experienced the loss of her nephew to an overdose, she understood the unique pain and confusion I was feeling. Randy, too, was steady and supportive, giving me the space to process while handling the practical tasks I couldn't yet face. Their love and understanding were lifelines in that moment of overwhelming despair.

Chapter 46: Logan's Final Hours

The detective provided more details about the events leading up to Logan's death, painting a picture that was both heartbreaking and frustrating. According to the roommate, they had smoked some weed and gone to bed around midnight. The simplicity of this statement belied the tragedy that followed. The detective also noted a puncture wound on the top of Logan's right hand, a detail that immediately raised questions. While no syringes or other paraphernalia related to heroin were found in the apartment, this puncture wound suggested something more had occurred.

The detective informed me that a large quantity of medical marijuana had been found in Logan's apartment. He had a medical marijuana card, and I knew he'd recently come into money, likely making a trip to the dispensary to stock up. That detail felt like a piece of Logan's personality, a mix of practicality and indulgence. But it also reminded me of how substances, even legal ones, played a central role in his life.

What troubled me most, though, was the lack of heroin related items in the apartment. Given Logan's history, this absence felt suspicious. I couldn't shake the thought that his roommate had sanitized the scene before calling 911, perhaps out of fear of legal repercussions. The detective seemed to share this suspicion, admitting that the roommate wasn't being entirely forthcoming. There was no doubt in my mind, or the detective's, that she knew more than she was letting on and was likely aware of exactly what had happened to Logan that night.

The puncture wound on Logan's hand raised a host of unsettling possibilities. Had someone else administered drugs to him? Was it an accident, or was it deliberate? Without the usual evidence, syringes, spoons, or residue, the details were murky, leaving more questions than answers. That single detail haunted me, representing not just what I didn't know but what I might never know about Logan's final hours.

The detective explained that the coroner would perform an autopsy to determine the official cause of death. While this was standard procedure, it didn't lessen the emotional weight of waiting for answers. She told me they would notify me when the body could be released, but that timeline felt impossibly long. I needed answers, needed to know what had happened to my son, but I also dreaded what those answers might reveal.

The roommate's role in this tragedy added a layer of complexity to my grief. On the one hand, I was furious at the thought that she might have altered the scene, potentially obscuring the truth. On the other hand, I couldn't ignore the reality of her fear in this situation. If she had sanitized the apartment, it was likely out of self-preservation, not malice. Still, her lack of honesty felt like a betrayal. Not just to me but to Logan.

Her actions, or lack thereof, also highlighted a harsh truth about addiction: it doesn't just affect the person using; it shapes the behaviors of those around them. Whether out of fear, denial, or self-interest, people in the orbit of addiction often make choices that complicate the pursuit of truth and justice.

In those couple of days, waiting for the autopsy results and the release of Logan's body, I felt utterly helpless. The uncertainty was suffocating, leaving me with nothing to do but replay the information I had over and over in my mind. The questions about what Logan's final moments had been like, whether he had been scared or alone, and what role his roommate had played consumed me.

Yet, amidst the chaos of my thoughts, I held onto the belief that I owed it to Logan to see this through and to gather as much truth as possible about what had happened and to honor his memory in whatever way I could. It was an unbearable weight, but it was one I had no choice but to carry.

Chapter 47: Grieving in Motion

After Logan's death, Randy told me that Steve and Laura had suggested canceling our planned camping trip. It was a kind and practical suggestion, given everything that had just happened. But with the weight of the global pandemic pressing down and the devastating loss of Logan fresh in my heart, I made the decision: we were still going camping.

The campground was close to home, and I was handling everything remotely anyway. I needed the peace and solitude that camping brought me. The quiet of the outdoors, the rhythm of setting up camp, and the simple act of being in nature felt like the only way I could find even a moment of stillness in the chaos of my grief.

I called the same funeral home in Sarasota that had handled Gina's and her parents' services. It felt strangely full-circle, though not in a way I had ever imagined or wanted. The funeral director was kind and compassionate, guiding me through the steps to have Logan cremated and his remains sent to Arkansas. Their understanding made a deeply painful process just a little easier to bear.

In those moments, I had to push aside the rawness of my emotions to focus on logistics. There were forms to sign, decisions to make, and steps to follow. It was surreal, arranging the cremation of my son while simultaneously preparing for a camping trip. But grief has no rulebook, and I was doing the best I could to keep moving forward.

The day after Logan's death, my father and his wife drove to Sarasota to help. They met with the detective, who gave them Logan's personal items that had been collected at the scene. My dad then went to Logan's apartment to see if anything else needed to be gathered. It was an act of love and support that I deeply appreciated, though I can only imagine how painful it was for him to walk into that space.

In the meantime, I had already notified Tammy. Our battle, our shared effort to support Logan through his addiction, had ended. I told her that her brothers, who lived in Sarasota, needed to pick up Gina's remains, which were still in Logan's apartment. Tammy, too, was devastated. Logan's death was a loss that rippled through everyone who had loved him, leaving grief and unanswered questions in its wake.

One of the hardest things to reconcile was my last conversation with Logan. It had been late the night before his death, just a quick call to check on him. He had been laughing, in good spirits, and having a good time. When I asked how he was doing, he said he couldn't talk right then but told me he loved me.

"I'll talk to you tomorrow," he said.

Those were his last words to me, and they haunt me. I'm still waiting for that call, the one that will never come. It's an ache that will never fully go away. A reminder of all the conversations we didn't get to have, all the things I didn't get to say, and all the moments we'll never share.

Camping became a strange but necessary refuge. The act of setting up the camper, sitting by the fire, and listening to the sounds of nature gave me space to process, even if just a little.

The campground's proximity to home meant I could handle calls and arrangements as needed, but being there also gave me a buffer from the overwhelming weight of grief.

Every now and then, I'd think about Logan's teasing, the way he used to say we weren't really camping because of all the comforts we brought along. I could almost hear his laugh, and feel his presence in the quiet moments. It brought a bittersweet sense of comfort, a reminder of his humor, and the love we shared, even in the midst of loss.

Logan's death left a hole in my heart that will never fully heal. The practical steps of making arrangements, the support from Randy and others, and the solitude of the campground were the threads I clung to in those first few days. But the grief, the unanswered questions, and the memory of his last words stay with me, a reminder of how fragile and precious life is.

Camping, in its quiet way, gave me a place to grieve without interruption, a way to be with my thoughts and memories of Logan. It wasn't an escape, but it was a way to keep moving, one small step at a time.

After the devastating news of Logan's death, I knew I needed support to navigate the storm of emotions and the practicalities that lay ahead. On that fateful Tuesday, I called Cindy, my lifelong friend, to tell her what had happened. Without hesitation, she made plans to join us at the campground that Friday afternoon. Her willingness to be there during such a traumatic experience brought me comfort even before she arrived.

Surprisingly, my friend Ann also decided she was coming to camp with us. She planned to sleep in her SUV, a gesture that showed just how much she cared. She didn't want me to face the weight of grief alone, and her presence felt like a quiet assurance that I had people in my corner.

The support didn't stop there. Our employees, who had always been like an extended family to us, banded together to express their sympathy. They brought a beautiful flower arrangement to the campground, a heartfelt gesture that reminded me how much we were loved and cared for. Even one of our client's daughters brought food for us, a delicious pasta salad that stands out in my memory. I've thought about that pasta salad so many times since, wishing I had more of it or at least the recipe.

These acts of kindness, big and small, were like beams of light cutting through the fog of grief. They reminded me that even in the darkest times, people show up for you in ways that matter.

That weekend at the campground, I leaned into the familiar routines of camping as a way to ground myself. As I always did on our trips, I took charge of most of the cooking. There was something soothing about the ritual of preparing meals, especially over an open fire in cast iron. The simplicity and focus it required gave me a brief respite from the overwhelming emotions swirling inside me.

We cooked, we ate, and we sat around the fire, listening to music and sharing stories. Much of the conversation centered on Logan, his humor, his charm, and the memories we all held of him. Talking about him brought both tears and laughter, a bittersweet mix that felt strangely healing. In the companionship of my friends and family, I found a small measure of peace.

That weekend wasn't about escaping grief but about leaning into the love and support that surrounded me. Cindy, Ann, Randy, Steve and Laura and others created a space where I could feel my emotions without judgment, where I could process the enormity of what had happened while also finding moments of joy in their presence.

There was something deeply comforting about sitting by the fire, the warmth and flicker of the flames reflecting the love and care I felt from those around me. The shared meals, the music, the conversations, they reminded me that while Logan's loss left an irreplaceable hole in my heart, I wasn't alone in carrying that weight.

That weekend at the campground became more than just a trip. It was a time of reflection, a chance to honor Logan in the company of people who loved and cared for me. It was a reminder of the strength that comes from the community and the way shared experiences, whether in grief or joy, can bring comfort when words alone fall short.

Chapter 48: A Father's Heartache

That Tuesday, when I spoke to my father about Logan's passing, I asked if he had talked to JD, my brother. He hadn't. He told me he was waiting for me to decide who to call and what to say. My father's understanding at that moment meant a lot. He let me take the lead, knowing this was a deeply personal and painful decision.

I knew I wanted to be the one to make that call. It wasn't something I could pass on to someone else. I called JD, and as soon as I started speaking, I could feel the weight of the words. I told him what had happened, and while the news devastated him, I sensed that he wasn't entirely surprised. Like me, he had likely lived with the quiet fear that this day might come, given Logan's struggles. That didn't make the loss any easier, but it brought an unspoken understanding between us.

After we talked, I asked JD to call my nieces and share the news with them. I just couldn't bring myself to be the one to deliver that blow. He agreed, and shortly after, I received messages from both of them. Their words were filled with sorrow, expressing how deeply they felt this loss and letting me know they loved me. Those messages meant the world to me.

They were a reminder of the bond our family shared and the love that remained, even in the face of such heartbreak.

In moments like these, family becomes a lifeline. The shared history, the mutual understanding of who Logan was and how much he meant to us, provided a small but meaningful comfort. JD's willingness to take on the difficult task of informing his daughters reflected the strength and compassion that runs through our family, even in our hardest moments.

The messages from my nieces reminded me that grief, though deeply personal, is also shared. Each of us lost something when we lost Logan, but we also gained the opportunity to lean on each other, express love and support, and honor his memory together.

When our camping trip ended on Sunday, we packed up the trailer, returned it to Ann's, and headed home. Walking into the house, I was struck by how surreal everything felt. The world around me was the same. Familiar and orderly. But inside, everything had changed. The loss of Logan was so profound, so life-altering, that it felt impossible to reconcile the normalcy of my surroundings with the chaos and grief in my heart.

In those moments, I felt a storm of emotions, anger, desperation, disbelief, and more anger, all mixed with a deep, aching sadness. My very belief in God was shaken to its core. How could a loving God allow this to happen? It felt unnatural, cruel, and impossibly unfair. A parent should never have to bury their child. It's an inversion of the natural order, a pain so profound it defies explanation.

I found myself questioning everything. If there was a God, how could He let Logan suffer the way he did? How could He take him from me, from the world? These were questions without answers, but they consumed me. The loss of Logan wasn't just a loss of my son, it felt like a loss of certainty, of faith, of the very foundation on which I'd built so much of my understanding of life.

In the midst of this turmoil, a memory surfaced, one so vivid that it brought me an unexpected sense of calm. I recalled hearing my great-grandmother wail after the death of my grandfather. She repeated, over and over, "A parent should not have to bury their child." Her grief was raw and primal, and as a child, it left a deep impression on me.

In the days since I'd learned of Logan's death, her words had replayed in my mind like a haunting refrain. But suddenly, as I stood in my home, I found a strange peace in remembering her. The sound of her sadness washed over me, not as a weight but as a connection, a reminder that this kind of grief, as unnatural and unbearable as it feels, is part of the human experience. I could almost hear her voice as if she were standing beside me, offering a kind of solidarity in sorrow.

That memory became an anchor. It didn't take away the pain, the anger, or the questions, but it gave me a sense of continuity. My great-grandmother's grief, my own, and the countless parents who have endured this unbearable loss. We were all part of a shared story, one that spans generations. There was something strangely comforting in that, a reminder that I wasn't alone in this pain.

Grief is chaotic, but in that moment, I found a small piece of order, a glimmer of peace amid the storm. The calmness wasn't about acceptance, because how can you ever truly accept something like this?, but about recognizing that even in the darkest times, there are threads of connection that hold us together.

As I stood there, reflecting on the surrealness of it all, I realized that moving forward wouldn't mean "getting over"

Logan's death. It would mean carrying it with me, weaving it into the fabric of my life, and finding ways to honor his memory. The questions, the anger, and the sadness would remain, but so would the love, the memories, and the small moments of peace, like the one my great-grandmother's words had given me.

Chapter 49: The Coroner's Call

A few days after Logan's passing, I received a call from the detective with updates from the coroner. The probable cause of death was listed as an overdose, though the exact determination would have to wait for toxicology reports, which could take several months due to backlogs. One detail stood out: the coroner had found that Logan had an enlarged heart, a condition likely caused by prolonged drug use. Hearing this only deepened my sadness. It was another reminder of how addiction had worn down his body and spirit over the years.

The detective also informed me that Logan's body was ready to be released and asked if I had a funeral home lined up. I provided the information for the funeral home in Sarasota, the same one that had handled Gina's and her parents' services.

When I called the funeral home to finalize arrangements, I was surprised to learn that Logan had not paid for his mother's services. The funeral home explained that in order to proceed with Logan's cremation, Gina's outstanding bill would need to be paid as well. I couldn't help but laugh at the irony. After years of being divorced, I found myself paying for Gina's memorial. It wasn't something I was upset about; in fact, it felt strangely fitting, a final act of connection between us.

I paid the bill without hesitation, glad to resolve something that had lingered unfinished. In a way, it felt like honoring both Gina and Logan, tying together the threads of their lives in a small but meaningful way.

Because we were in the middle of the COVID-19 pandemic, I had to handle all the arrangements remotely from Arkansas. Even something as personal as choosing the container for Logan's remains was done from a distance. It was surreal, picking out a box to hold the ashes of my son, reduced to a physical form I could hardly bear to think about.

The funeral home moved quickly, collecting Logan's body, performing the cremation, and shipping the remains. I asked them to send the package to Ann's house, unsure if I would be home to receive it. It felt strange to plan something so final for Logan without being able to be present, but the pandemic had made everything about grief and mourning more complicated.

One day, Ann called me and said, "Logan's here." The words hit me hard. I immediately got in the car with Randy, and we drove to Ann's house to pick up the package. I didn't know what to expect when I held the box for the first time, but I was struck by how heavy it was.

My son, so full of life, laughter, and love was now reduced to ashes inside an oak box with his name and dates engraved on it. The finality of it all was overwhelming. Holding that box, I felt the weight of both the wood and the grief, each pressing on my heart in a way I could never have imagined.

The pandemic complicated every aspect of mourning. I made the difficult decision to delay planning a memorial service. I didn't want to risk exposing my father, who was in a vulnerable age group, to the dangers of flying or gathering in a crowd. At the time of writing this, I still haven't held a memorial service for Logan, and I'm not sure I ever will.

There's a part of me that doesn't want to reopen those wounds, to relive the pain in such a public way. But I know how much Logan meant to so many people. Gina's family, my family, and friends from all parts of our lives were ready and willing to gather, even at the height of the pandemic, to honor Logan's memory. Their love and willingness to take that risk spoke volumes about the impact Logan had on those who knew him.

Not having a formal service has left me in a state of incomplete mourning. While I've found ways to honor Logan in private moments, there's a lingering feeling of unfinished business. Grief is a journey with no clear path, and for me, it has been about finding peace in the small ways I can remember Logan; through stories, laughter, and the quiet moments where I feel his presence most strongly.

Holding that oak box, bringing Logan home, and knowing that he was back with me, in some way, brought a measure of comfort. But the ache of his absence, the questions that remain unanswered, and the rituals of mourning left undone will always be a part of my journey.

After Logan's death, figuring out how to move forward became an urgent need. The weight of my grief was unbearable, and I knew I couldn't navigate it alone. A sense of urgency haunted me, pushing me to find someone who could guide me through the profound sadness and confusion I was feeling.

I reached out to a social worker I was familiar with through my business. She was compassionate and understanding, and she promised to help. True to her word, she connected me with a local hospice organization that hosted grief support groups. That connection changed everything.

Chapter 50: Grief

I received a call from Simone and Jamie, facilitators of a newly organized grief support group meeting via Zoom due to the pandemic. They invited me to join, and though I was unsure of what to expect, I felt a glimmer of hope. My heart was breaking, and I desperately needed a space to express my sorrow and confusion without judgment.

From the very first meeting, I knew I had found something special. The group, facilitated by Simone and Jamie, created a safe and accepting environment. They didn't offer clichés or insist on a roadmap to "get over it." Instead, they listened. They acknowledged my pain, encouraged me to lean into the grief, and assured me that there was no right or wrong way to mourn.

One of the most powerful lessons I learned in those early meetings was that grief has no end. It's not something you "fix" or "move on" from; it's something you learn to carry. They encouraged me to embrace my sorrow, to lean into the pain rather than avoid it. As difficult and counterintuitive as it seemed, I found comfort in hearing that the overwhelming weight I felt wasn't something to be conquered but something to live with.

The facilitators and the group members assured me that while the pain would never fully go away, it would become easier to carry with time. They emphasized that grief is deeply personal. There's no standardized plan, no timeline, and no need to compare my process to anyone else's. It was a revelation to hear this, a permission slip to grieve in my own way and at my own pace.

The group became a lifeline. Twice a week in the beginning, and later once a week for about six months, I joined those meetings. Whether I was at home, at the office, or even at a campground, I made time to connect with the group. Some days I listened quietly, absorbing the stories of others who had experienced loss. On other days, I shared my own pain, my memories of Logan, and my struggles to find meaning and direction.

What stood out most was the sense of community. These were people who understood, in a way no one else could, what it felt like losing someone you love. They knew the hollow ache of missing someone, the moments of anger and disbelief, and the bittersweet comfort of cherished memories. Their understanding helped me feel less alone, even in the depths of my grief.

Though the group couldn't take away my pain, it gave me some tools to navigate it. I learned that grief doesn't follow a straight line; it ebbs and flows, sometimes overwhelming and sometimes quiet. I also learned that it was okay to feel joy again, to laugh, and to find moments of peace without betraying Logan's memory.

The lessons I took from those meetings continue to guide me. I carry Logan's memory with me every day, and while the grief is always there, it no longer feels like it's swallowing me whole. It's a part of me, woven into the fabric of my life, but it doesn't define me.

Chapter 51: Life After Logan

After Logan's death, everything in my life changed. The loss felt like a seismic shift, leaving me more withdrawn, confused, and weighed down by sadness. Depression crept in, mingled with bouts of anger I didn't always know how to express or direct. Each day felt like a battle to process those raw emotions and find even the faintest thread of normalcy.

One of the most puzzling and painful aspects of this journey has been the silence. People avoid saying Logan's name out loud, as though it's too fragile to be spoken or might shatter me if uttered. The caution and hesitation in their voices, when topics of addiction or loss come up, are palpable. It's as though they're tiptoeing around a landmine, afraid of triggering something in me. But the truth is, all I want is for Logan's name to be spoken out loud.

When a child dies, one of the most profound fears for a parent is that their child will be forgotten. I want people to remember Logan. Not just his death, but his life. His laughter, his charm, his quirks, the stories that made him who he was. Logan's death, though tragic, doesn't define him. It was unintended, a cruel and senseless ending to a life that held so much more.

I long for family and friends to share stories that include Logan, and to reminisce about moments when he was vibrant and alive. When they don't, the silence feels like another loss, as though even his memory is slipping away. Speaking his name isn't a reminder of pain, it's a reminder of love, of his impact, of the life he lived.

When the toxicology report came back months later, it confirmed what we had expected: Logan had died of an overdose due to fentanyl poisoning. I asked about the amount of fentanyl in his system. What I do remember is the coroner telling me it was enough to kill him but not enough to suggest he had intentionally taken his own life.

That distinction brought a strange kind of relief. It was an accident, not a choice to leave this world. Fentanyl is ruthless, potent enough to kill in tiny amounts, and it has turned the drug supply into a deadly minefield. Logan didn't stand a chance against it, like so many others who unknowingly consume substances laced with this poison.

The caution people show around me is likely well-meaning, but it only deepens my isolation. Avoiding Logan's name or the topic of addiction doesn't protect me from pain, it amplifies it. It makes me feel like I'm carrying his memory alone like his life is being erased in the name of sparing my feelings. What I truly need is for those who loved him, and even those who didn't know him well, to talk about him. To laugh about his jokes, to remember his quirks, to keep his spirit alive through stories.

Logan's death doesn't define him. Yes, it's part of his story, but it's not the whole story. He was so much more than his addiction or the circumstances of his passing. He was a son, a friend, a nephew, and a person full of life and potential. Remembering him means embracing all of those parts, not just the tragic ending. I refuse to let the circumstances surrounding his death define him.

Learning to live with the grief of losing Logan is an ongoing process. It's not something I'll ever "get over," but it's something I'm learning to carry. Part of that journey is finding ways to ensure Logan isn't forgotten. Whether through telling his story, sharing his name, or raising awareness about fentanyl and Substance Use Disorder, I want to honor his memory in a way that feels true to who he was.

The Zoom support group meetings I attended in the months after Logan's death were invaluable. Simone and Jamie created a space where I could process my grief without judgment, and I will forever be grateful for their guidance. But as helpful as those meetings were, the group was made up of people whose losses were varied, spouses, siblings, parents and none of them had lost a child to an overdose or fentanyl poisoning.

I found myself needing more answers. I needed to understand addiction and the devastating impact of fentanyl. I was searching for a community, people who had walked the same path, who could help me make sense of the senseless. That search became a new focus, a way to channel my grief into something purposeful.

Chapter 52: Bridging the Gap

In August of 2022, Ann told me about an event being held in downtown Little Rock at the Clinton Presidential Library. It was scheduled for August 31st, National Overdose Awareness Day, and was called "Bridge the Gap." Ann sent me the information, and I was immediately intrigued. The event requested attendees to bring donations of socks, T-shirts, and underwear, new and in any size or amount, for people in recovery. It was a small gesture, but one that felt meaningful, so I went out and bought as much as I could.

The event had another draw: Bill Clinton himself was scheduled to speak. Having lived in Arkansas for many years, I'd met him and Hillary on a few occasions through mutual connections. My cousins had gone to college with the Clintons and remained friends over the years. I was curious to hear what he had to say about overdose deaths and addiction, topics that felt so personal and urgent to me.

As I gathered the donations and prepared to attend, I felt a mix of anticipation and apprehension. I didn't know what I would discover at this event, but I hoped it might bring me closer to the answers and the community I was seeking. I wanted to understand more about addiction, about fentanyl, and about what could be done to prevent other families from enduring the kind of loss I had experienced.

This event felt like a step toward something bigger, a way to honor Logan's memory by learning and connecting. It was also a way to channel the restless energy that grief had left in me, an urgency to do something even when I didn't yet know what that something would be.

Attending "Bridge the Gap" wasn't just about learning, it was about finding a sense of purpose in the face of profound loss. It marked the beginning of a new chapter in my grief journey, one where I began to see how Logan's story could help raise awareness and possibly save lives. While I didn't yet know how, I felt this event might point me in the right direction.

When August 31st arrived, it carried with it a mix of emotions, anticipation, nervousness, and a sense of longing for connection. Randy and I gathered the donation items we had collected, dressed for the sweltering Arkansas heat, and drove to the Clinton Presidential Library to attend the event. As we arrived, we saw a few hundred people milling around, some dropping off clothing donations, others talking quietly among themselves. Randy and I stood off to the side, trying to take it all in. At that moment, I still wasn't sure what to expect.

As the event began, presenters shared their stories of addiction and recovery. Each story was deeply personal, filled with raw emotion and resilience. Then, a fiery and passionate woman named Staci stepped forward to speak. She told the story of her son, Hagen, who had died after taking a counterfeit pill laced with illicit fentanyl. Hagen's death had ignited something powerful in Staci, propelling her to raise awareness about the dangers of fentanyl and opioids. Her passion and drive were palpable, and I felt an instant connection to her mission.

Staci had founded a group called the Hope Movement Coalition, dedicated to education, advocacy, and honoring those lost to this crisis. As she spoke, I could feel the fire of her determination, and it resonated deeply with me. I knew her story and her cause were something I needed to be part of.

After the presentations, the crowd gathered at the base of the walking bridge that spans the Arkansas River, connecting the Clinton Library to North Little Rock. Photographers captured the moment, even using a drone for a group photo. As the group began walking up onto the bridge, Staci explained that it was lined with banners, tributes from groups like Lost Voices of Fentanyl and Can You See Me Now. Each banner bore the faces of people lost to overdose or fentanyl poisoning, their lives memorialized in photos that told stories of love, loss, and tragedy.

As I ascended the bridge, surrounded by hundreds of others who had also lost loved ones, I felt an overwhelming mix of emotions. I realized these were my people, others who understood the pain I carried, the longing to see their loved ones remembered, and the drive to prevent further losses.

The sight of the banners was staggering. There were over 50 of them, each holding the faces of 50 to 100 people, thousands of lives represented in one place. Walking past those banners, seeing the faces of sons, daughters, mothers, fathers, friends, and siblings, was almost too much to bear. My pace slowed as my heart raced, and my breath caught in my chest. The weight of it all was suffocating, but I remembered what Simone and Jamie had taught me: Lean into those feelings.

And I did. I let the grief and the love wash over me, allowing myself to truly feel the magnitude of what I was witnessing. It was simultaneously one of the most beautiful and most heartbreaking experiences of my life, a profound mix of community and loss, joy and sadness.

In the center of the bridge, a microphone had been set up. Staci gathered the group's attention and began to speak again, her voice carrying the weight of both sorrow and determination.

She acknowledged the faces on the banners, recognizing them as our loved ones. Then she began reading the names of those who had died from overdose and fentanyl poisoning.

As dusk fell, the bridge lights came on, glowing a vibrant purple in honor of those we had lost. Music played, and the atmosphere was both somber and hopeful. I stood there, surrounded by hundreds of people, and found myself sobbing like a child. The grief I had carried so silently for so long found a release in that moment, surrounded by others who truly understood.

Afterward, I knew I had to meet Staci. I approached her to thank her for what she was doing and to ask if Logan's name could be included the next time. Without hesitation, she pulled out a piece of paper and wrote his name down. Her kindness and immediacy made me feel seen, and for the first time in a long time, I felt a sense of belonging.

These were my people. This was my community. In their stories, their tears, and their shared mission, I found a place where Logan's life and death could be honored and where I could channel my grief into something meaningful. It wasn't just an event; it was a turning point, a moment where I began to see how I could move forward while carrying Logan's memory with me.

Before attending my first Bridge the Gap event, I felt utterly alone in my struggle to understand Logan's senseless death.

Losing a child to overdose or fentanyl poisoning comes with a unique and heavy burden. Not just the grief, but the stigma that surrounds it. People don't talk about it. The silence is deafening, and isolating, and it keeps so many of us from finding the support we desperately need.

I didn't know where to turn, and I didn't think anyone else could truly understand what I was feeling. But Staci, with her passion and determination, had found a way to break through that silence. She gathered people like me, people who carried the same kind of pain, and brought us together. Standing on that bridge, surrounded by complete strangers, I experienced something I never expected: unconditional love and camaraderie.

Everyone on that bridge had suffered a loss. Some had already placed their loved ones' faces on the banners, while others, like me, were just beginning to understand this new and painful reality. As I stood there, tears streaming down my face, people I didn't know, complete strangers, wrapped me in their arms and told me they understood. They didn't just say it; they meant it. Their words weren't empty or obligatory, they came from a place of lived experience.

At that moment, I realized I am not alone. It was overwhelming but also comforting in a way I hadn't thought possible. For the first time, I felt like I was part of a community that truly understood the depth of my pain. These were people who knew what it meant to grieve a loved one lost to overdose or fentanyl poisoning. They weren't afraid to speak about it, to cry about it, to embrace the rawness of it all.

The stigma surrounding overdose deaths keeps so many families in the shadows, afraid to speak openly about their loss. It isolates us, making an already unbearable grief feel even heavier. But standing on that bridge, the stigma faded away. It was replaced by a sense of shared humanity, a collective recognition that our loved ones mattered, that their stories deserved to be told.

Staci's ability to bring us together was nothing short of remarkable. She created a space where we could mourn without judgment, where we could cry and share and remember our loved ones for who they truly were, not just their struggles, but their lives, their love, their light.

That day on the bridge was a turning point for me. For the first time since Logan's death, I felt seen and heard in a way I hadn't before. The hugs, the kind words, the tears we shared reminded me that while the pain of losing Logan will never go away, I don't have to carry it alone. There is a community of people who understand, who are walking the same path, and who are ready to stand with me in the fight to end the stigma and raise awareness.

Months after attending Bridge the Gap, I discovered the group's Facebook page. It felt like a lifeline, a space where stories like Logan's were shared, connections were made, and the stigma of overdose deaths was dismantled. I quickly made a request to join and was approved. One of the first things I noticed was an announcement about monthly meetings held at a pizza place in North Little Rock on the last Saturday of every month. I had no idea what to expect, but Randy and I decided to go.

When we walked into the private dining area that first time, I was immediately greeted by familiar faces, people I recognized from Bridge the Gap. They walked up to us, hugged me, and told us how happy they were that we'd come. That warmth and kindness meant everything in that moment. It was another reminder that this was a community where Logan and I both belonged, where his story and my grief were understood without explanation or judgment.

We found our seats, unsure of what was to come but ready to lean into the experience. The smell of pizza filled the room, and the casual setting offered a surprising contrast to the heavy emotions being carried by everyone present. This wasn't just a room full of grieving people; it was a room full of strength, resilience, and purpose.

As the meeting began, the group made a few announcements, and then we went around the room to introduce ourselves and share about our loved ones. Listening to the introductions was humbling and heartbreaking. These weren't just stories of loss; they were stories of love, of lives cut short, and of people fighting to make their grief mean something.

One mother had lost two of her children to overdose, one of them on Mother's Day. The fact that she could sit there, share her story, and advocate for change was a testament to her strength and resolve. Each person in that room had faced unimaginable pain, yet they were there, supporting one another and working to raise awareness.

When it was my turn, I introduced Randy and myself, and then the words caught in my throat. It was the first time I'd spoken about Logan's death in public, and the weight of saying it out loud was almost too much to bear. I struggled to speak his name, let alone tell his story, but no one in that room rushed me or made me feel like I had to hurry. Instead, there was only an outpouring of love and compassion.

The room was silent as I gathered myself, tears streaming down my face. It was okay that I was struggling; it was understood. This wasn't a place for polished speeches or rehearsed words; it was a place for raw emotion, honesty, and connection. Eventually, I managed to say his name and share a little about him. Though it felt like breaking open a wound, it also felt like honoring him.

Although it was hard to speak that day, it was another turning point. I had found a community where it was okay to grieve openly, to struggle with the words, and to lean on others for support. These were people who had walked a similar path and who understood the weight of the loss I carried.

Over time, I've become more comfortable telling Logan's story. I still get choked up, and I probably always will, but I do it anyway. Because his story matters. Because his life mattered. And because sharing it helps keep his memory alive while also raising awareness about the dangers of fentanyl and addiction.

That first meeting showed me that healing doesn't mean forgetting, and strength doesn't mean hiding your pain. It's about finding ways to carry your grief while also finding purpose in it. Logan's story has become part of my purpose, and this community has given me the strength to tell it.

One of the most meaningful steps I took in honoring Logan's memory was submitting his picture to be included on the Can You See Me Now banners. When I learned his photo had been added to Banner 31, I felt a mix of emotions and pride that his life was being acknowledged, sorrow that his face now stood among so many others lost to fentanyl, and a fierce determination to make sure his story helped raise awareness.

These banners, along with the Lost Voices of Fentanyl banners, appear at rallies across the United States, including in Washington, D.C. They serve as a visual reminder of the devastating toll fentanyl poisoning has taken on families like mine. Seeing Logan's face on one of these banners felt surreal. It was both a memorial to him and a call to action for others, a demand to recognize the scale of this crisis and the urgent need for change.

The banners are powerful in their simplicity. Each one holds the faces of dozens of loved ones, representing lives cut tragically short by overdose or fentanyl poisoning. Together, they send an undeniable message: this is not an isolated problem. It's a nationwide crisis, an epidemic affecting families in every community, every state and from every walk of life.

For me, the banners make the issue personal. They transform statistics into stories, faces, and names. They show that these aren't just "overdose deaths"; these are sons, daughters, siblings, parents, and friends whose lives were stolen by SUD and the deadly proliferation of fentanyl-laced drugs.

At rallies and events, the banners are more than just tributes, they are tools for advocacy. They bring visibility to a crisis that often remains hidden behind stigma and silence. By displaying the faces of those we've lost, they challenge people to confront the reality of the opioid epidemic and the dangers of fentanyl.

Fentanyl, a synthetic opioid 50 to 100 times more potent than morphine, has become a silent killer. It's found in nearly every street drug, from counterfeit pills to cocaine, heroin, and even marijuana. These banners help drive home the fact that this is an attack on our communities. It's not just an addiction problem; it's a poisoning crisis, and every family is at risk.

Having Logan on Banner 31 is a way of ensuring his life, and his death, become part of a larger movement to save lives. It's a way of saying, He mattered. His story matters. It's also a way for me to channel my grief into action, to stand with others who are fighting to raise awareness and push for change.

I hope that by sharing Logan's story and seeing his face among the thousands of others, people will understand that this isn't just a problem for "other people." It's a problem that affects all of us, and it demands our attention and action.

The banners are a powerful reminder that this fight is far from over. They're a call to action for better education about the dangers of fentanyl, more robust addiction treatment options, and stronger measures to prevent these drugs from flooding our communities. For me, they're also a way of keeping Logan's memory alive while working to ensure that no other family has to endure this kind of loss.

Attending meetings and events like Bridge the Gap and monthly gatherings, it became obvious that the majority of participants were moms. It wasn't that fathers weren't grieving, they absolutely were. But for some reason, men seemed less visible in these spaces. I started to wonder: Where are the dads?

It's likely that stigma plays a significant role. Society often expects men to be stoic, to avoid showing vulnerability, especially when it comes to emotions as raw and overwhelming as grief. Many dads may feel pressure to remain strong for their families, to bury their pain and "carry on" rather than confront it openly. This cultural expectation can create a barrier that keeps men from seeking support or even acknowledging their grief fully.

For me, that wasn't an option. I couldn't and wouldn't suppress my emotions. I wanted to be a face in this fight, a man unafraid to say, "This is my son, this is my pain, and this is our story".

Grief is deeply personal, and no two people experience it the same way. However, there are patterns in how men and women tend to process grief, often influenced by societal expectations, upbringing, and personal coping mechanisms.

Women are often more likely to express their grief openly. They might cry, talk about their feelings, and seek support from friends, family, or community groups. Women often find comfort in sharing their stories and connecting with others who have experienced similar losses.

Men, on the other hand, are more likely to contain their emotions. They might avoid talking about their grief or showing outward signs of vulnerability. Instead, they often channel their feelings into action, working harder, taking on projects, or focusing on problem-solving as a way to cope. This doesn't mean men feel less; they just process and express grief differently.

Women are more likely to seek out support groups, therapy, or other communal forms of healing. Sharing their grief can feel validating and help them process their emotions in a safe space.

Men are less likely to seek out formal support. They may internalize their pain, fearing that sharing it would make them appear weak or incapable. As a result, they might isolate themselves, even when they desperately need connection and understanding.

While women also take action in response to loss, advocating, organizing events, or raising awareness, they tend to balance action with emotional expression.

Men often lean heavily into action as a coping mechanism. They might focus on fixing problems, creating solutions, or honoring their loved ones in tangible ways. For some, this is a way to channel their grief; for others, it's a way to avoid confronting their emotions head-on.

The lack of dads in these groups is a stark reminder of how pervasive the stigma surrounding grief, and especially grief related to addiction and overdose, can be. Men are often conditioned to believe that vulnerability equals weakness and that showing emotion is somehow unmanly. This cultural narrative needs to change.

Seeing other men openly grieving and advocating can help break down the barriers that keep fathers from participating. When men like me show up, speak out, and share our stories, it sends a message: It's okay to feel. It's okay to grieve. And it's okay to do it publicly.

While many support groups naturally attract more women, creating spaces specifically for men, where they can process their grief in ways that feel comfortable for them, could make a significant difference.

Changing the narrative around masculinity and vulnerability is key. Men need to hear, from other men, that it's not only okay to grieve openly, it's necessary for healing.

By stepping into these spaces and sharing Logan's story, I hope to contribute to this shift. I want to be a visible reminder that fathers grieve too, that their pain is valid, and that there is strength in vulnerability. Losing Logan to fentanyl poisoning is a pain I'll carry for the rest of my life, but by sharing it, I can honor his memory and help others find the courage to confront their own grief.

One of the most striking realizations I've had while attending these meetings and becoming more involved in the fight against fentanyl poisoning is the sheer number of people in recovery who are also mourning the loss of a loved one to substance use disorder. It's unimaginable to me, the strength and resilience it must take to stay on the path of recovery while carrying the heavy burden of grief.

Grieving the loss of a child to addiction is already one of the most profound and isolating experiences a person can endure. Add to that the daily struggle of staying sober, of working through the triggers, cravings, and emotional landmines that come with recovery, and it's a testament to their courage that these individuals are able to get out of bed every morning.

I can't help but feel awe and admiration for those in recovery who are navigating both their own healing and the loss of someone they loved deeply. Recovery is a monumental task on its own, requiring immense self-awareness, commitment, and strength. Grief, particularly the grief of losing a child, adds another layer of complexity, often shaking the very foundation of a person's mental and emotional wellness.

Every time I meet someone in recovery, I celebrate their journey. Their willingness to take control of their mental wellness and remain sober, even in the face of unimaginable pain, is an inspiration. It's proof of the human spirit's capacity to endure, to rebuild, and to find purpose in the face of tragedy.

No amount of storytelling will bring Logan back. That's a truth I've come to accept, as painful as it is. But if sharing Logan's story, our story, can help even one person, it's worth it. If hearing about the pain left behind by survivors helps someone recognize the stakes, motivates them to seek help, or reinforces their commitment to recovery, then telling Logan's story becomes more than just a tribute to him. It becomes a lifeline for someone else.

I've come to see storytelling as an act of hope and healing. It's about creating connection and understanding, about showing others that they're not alone in their struggles. Logan's story, like so many others, is a reminder of the dangers of addiction but also of the love, light, and humanity that addiction so often obscures.

Every person in recovery has the potential to create a ripple effect. Their healing not only transforms their own life but also touches the lives of those around them; family, friends, and even strangers who hear their stories. In the same way, telling Logan's story creates its own ripples. It's not just about raising awareness of the dangers of fentanyl; it's about fostering compassion, reducing stigma, and offering hope to those still fighting their battles.

I hope that Logan's story helps others see that recovery is not just about overcoming addiction, it's about reclaiming life, love, and connection. And for those in recovery who have also faced loss, it's about proving that it's possible to honor their loved one's memory while building a future of their own.

So, I'll keep telling Logan's story. I'll tell it at meetings, at rallies, to friends and strangers alike. Because if his story can save even one life, inspire someone to seek help, or show someone in recovery that their efforts matter, then his memory lives on in the most meaningful way.

As Bridge the Gap 2023 approached, my perspective and understanding of addiction, overdose, and fentanyl poisoning had grown significantly. The conversations about how illicit fentanyl was making its way into the country were everywhere, often focusing on the southern border. While I understood the concern, I also recognized that the issue was far more complex than any one cause or solution. This nuance shaped how I approached the event, ready to engage with the larger mission while holding onto my personal focus: Logan.

This time, I attended with more optimism and focus. I knew what to expect, but the emotions still felt unpredictable. Once again, the Clinton Presidential Library grounds served as the backdrop, with the bridge lined with banners bearing the faces of our loved ones, a hauntingly beautiful tribute to lives cut short.

As the presentations wrapped up, Staci once again stood before the crowd, her presence commanding and compassionate. She spoke about the bridge, the banners, and what it meant to walk among the faces of our loved ones. For those of us who had added pictures since the last event, she explained what we would see and feel, gently preparing us for the emotional journey ahead.

Walking onto the bridge, I knew Logan's face was there, waiting for me. Still, nothing could have prepared me for the moment I found his picture. My beautiful son, smiling back at me among the hundreds of faces of others who had died in the same senseless way.

Seeing him there was both comforting and devastating. It was a reminder that he wasn't alone in his struggle, but it also drove home the permanence of his absence. Grief washed over me as it always does, and all I could do was cry. The mix of love, sorrow, and pride was overwhelming, and I let the tears come, knowing they were part of the process.

As I gathered myself, I listened to Staci speak on the bridge. Her words were powerful, filled with both grief and determination. She reminded us why we were there. Not just to mourn, but to honor and to fight for awareness and change.

Then she began reading names, starting with her own son. Her voice carried the weight of every parent, sibling, and friend who had lost someone. And then, clear and loud over the speaker system, I heard her say, Logan Ballinger.

Hearing his name spoken aloud, in front of thousands of people, was a moment I'll never forget. It was an acknowledgment of his life, his story, and his place in this community. For a brief moment, it felt like Logan was there with me, his presence tangible among the faces and voices of those who loved and missed him.

That simple act of saying his name meant everything. It was a reminder that Logan mattered, that his life was seen and remembered. In a world that so often avoids speaking the names of those lost to addiction, this public recognition was an invaluable gift. It validated his life and his struggle while bringing his memory into a space of collective love and mourning.

Bridge the Gap 2023 reinforced for me that grief is not a solitary journey. It's shared, carried together by those who understand its weight. Logan's picture on that bridge, his name spoken aloud, and the community surrounding me all reaffirmed my commitment to telling his story and fighting for awareness.

After the Bridge the Gap 2023 event, I found myself stepping back from the monthly meetings. My concerns about the political tone of one speaker had left me uneasy, and I wasn't sure if the group was the right fit for me anymore. But then one day, my phone rang, it was Staci.

She wanted to know if I was okay, where I'd been, and why I had stopped attending the meetings. Her genuine concern struck a chord with me. When I shared my worries about the political speech, she immediately reassured me. "It's not about politics," she said firmly. "This is about raising awareness, honoring our loved ones, and fighting to save lives."

Her words reminded me of the core mission of the group and why I had felt so connected to it in the first place. Staci's outreach was heartfelt and unwavering, and she asked me to give the meetings another chance. I agreed, and Randy and I went to the very next one.

I can't tell you how glad I am that Staci made that call. Walking back into that room, being embraced by the community again, felt like coming home. It reminded me why this work is so important and how vital it is to be part of something bigger than my grief.

At one of the meetings in the months leading up to Bridge the Gap 2024, the group discussed the need to raise funds to continue the incredible work the Hope Movement Coalition was doing. For the first time, the Bridge the Gap event would also serve as a fundraiser, helping to sustain the organization's mission of awareness, support, and advocacy.

When the call went out for volunteers to help, I felt compelled to step up. I offered to approach businesses and connections in Little Rock, Arkansas, to ask for sponsorships and donations for the cause. It wasn't easy, it meant telling Logan's story over and over again, each time peeling back the layers of my grief to share the pain and the purpose behind it. But I quickly realized that sharing his story was incredibly powerful.

Every time I told Logan's story, it resonated with people. While it was tough to relive the details of his life and loss, it was also deeply rewarding to see how it opened people's hearts and minds. Many of the people I approached were willing to help. They saw the importance of the work we were doing and wanted to be part of the solution.

Logan's story became a bridge, not just between my grief and action but between the community and this vital cause. People who had never considered the impact of fentanyl or addiction began to understand the urgency and the human cost.

One of the most meaningful contributions came from my father. He sent a donation through our family nonprofit, Help the Least of These, honoring Logan's memory and supporting the work of the Hope Movement Coalition. His gesture was a powerful reminder that this fight isn't just mine, it's shared by those who love me and who loved Logan.

As my involvement deepened, I found myself making connections, building relationships, and bringing in much needed support for the coalition. Before long, I was asked to asked to be more active in the Hope Movement Coalition. It was an honor I didn't take lightly.

Being on the board gave me an even greater sense of purpose. It wasn't just about fundraising or organizing events, it was about shaping the mission, amplifying voices, and ensuring that the stories of our loved ones were not forgotten. I was no longer just a grieving parent; I was part of a movement to create change.

Returning to the meetings, volunteering, and joining the board have been transformative. They've given me a way to channel my grief into action, to honor Logan in a way that feels meaningful and impactful. Through this work, I've found a renewed sense of connection, not just to Logan's memory but to the broader community fighting this crisis.

Chapter 53: Carrying Logan's Story

Writing this book has been one of the most difficult things I've ever done. Reopening wounds, reliving memories, and revisiting the stories of Logan's life, both the joyful moments and the times of great struggle, has been a deeply emotional process. But it's also been necessary. Telling Logan's story is my mission now, and through this book, I hope his life and legacy will touch the hearts and minds of those who read it.

Logan's story is not just his own; it's part of a much larger crisis that demands our attention. Every day, our youth are under attack by illicit fentanyl. While there's much debate about how it enters our country it's clear that fentanyl has infiltrated communities in every corner of our nation.

But this crisis isn't just about stopping the flow of fentanyl. It's about addressing the systemic issues that fuel addiction and overdose in the first place. It's about mental wellness, awareness, and prevention. And most of all, it's about breaking the stigma that surrounds substance use disorder.

Fentanyl is everywhere. It's laced into counterfeit pills, heroin, cocaine, and even marijuana, and it's killing people at an alarming rate. Many young people don't even know they're taking it, believing they're using something "safe," only to have their lives tragically cut short.

We need to start conversations with those we love, especially young people, about the dangers of fentanyl and opioids. Social media has become a powerful influence, both good and bad, on the younger generation. While it can connect people to resources and support, it also exposes them to misinformation, peer pressure, and the glamorization of risky behaviors. Parents, educators, and mentors must step in to educate, guide, and protect.

One of the greatest barriers to addressing substance use disorder is the stigma that surrounds it. Too often, addiction is seen as a moral failing or a choice rather than the complex, multifaceted disease that it is. This stigma isolates those who are struggling, making them less likely to seek help, and it silences families who have experienced loss, leaving them to grieve in shame and solitude.

Here's how we can stop the stigma:

- Speak Openly and Honestly: Talk about substance use disorder and addiction as you would any other health issue.

- Share stories of recovery and resilience, and remember that every person struggling with addiction is someone's child, parent, sibling, or friend.

- Use Compassionate Language: Words matter. Replace terms like "addict" or "junkie" with "person with substance use disorder." This simple shift recognizes the humanity of those affected and frames addiction as a condition, not a character flaw.

- Educate Yourself and Others: Learn about addiction, its causes, and its treatment. Share that knowledge with your community to dispel myths and misinformation.

- Support Recovery Efforts: Advocate for better access to treatment, mental health care, and harm reduction programs. Celebrate those in recovery and recognize their strength and determination.

- Honor Those We've Lost: Remembering and talking about those who have died from overdose is a powerful way to break the silence. Sharing their stories keeps their memories alive and raises awareness about the urgent need for change.

This isn't a battle that can be fought alone. It requires a collective effort from individuals, families, communities, and policymakers. It requires funding for mental health services, education programs, and addiction treatment facilities. It requires compassion and understanding for those who are struggling, and it requires vigilance to protect our youth from the dangers they face.

Logan's story is just one of thousands, but it's a reminder that every life lost to this crisis is a life that mattered. By sharing his story, I hope to spark conversations, inspire action, and contribute to a future where fewer families have to endure this pain.

To those reading this book, I leave you with this: Be part of the solution. Talk to your children, your friends, and your community. Educate yourself about the dangers of fentanyl and opioids. Support policies and programs that address mental wellness and substance use disorder. And most importantly, show compassion. Let's create a world where addiction isn't hidden in shame but confronted with understanding and support.

Logan's story doesn't end here. It continues through every life it touches, every conversation it sparks, and every action it inspires. Together, we can make a difference.

Let's honor those we've lost by fighting for those still here. Let's end the stigma and save lives.

Chapter 54: Changing the Narrative

To create a future where fewer lives are lost to addiction and fentanyl poisoning, we must change the narrative surrounding substance use. Addiction is not a moral failing or a lack of willpower, it is a disease. By understanding this and working together, we can create an environment that fosters recovery, saves lives, and offers hope without judgment or criticism.

Addiction is recognized as a chronic brain disease by the medical community, including the National Institute on Drug Abuse (NIDA). It changes how the brain functions, affecting areas responsible for decision-making, impulse control, and reward. While the initial decision to use a substance might be voluntary for some, the progression into addiction involves complex interactions between genetics, mental health, environment, and brain chemistry.

This understanding is crucial to ending the stigma. People struggling with addiction are not weak or immoral, they are living with a disease that requires treatment, compassion, and support, just like diabetes, heart disease, or cancer.

Fentanyl is a synthetic opioid that is 50 to 100 times more potent than morphine. Originally developed for medical use in severe pain management, its illicit counterpart has flooded the drug supply, worsening the opioid crisis.

Key Statistics:

- Fentanyl-related deaths have skyrocketed in recent years. In the United States, fentanyl was involved in over 75,000 overdose deaths in 2022, a staggering increase compared to previous years.

- In 2021, fentanyl became the leading cause of death for adults aged 18–45 in the U.S., surpassing car accidents, suicide, and gun violence.

- Even trace amounts of fentanyl, equivalent to a few grains of salt, can be fatal. Its potency makes it particularly dangerous, as users often have no idea they are consuming it.

- Fentanyl is often mixed with other drugs like heroin, cocaine, or counterfeit pills, with users unaware of its presence. This unpredictability leads to accidental overdoses.

- Just 2 milligrams of fentanyl can be lethal. Its potency makes it far more dangerous than other opioids, leaving little room for error.

- Fentanyl works quickly, often overwhelming the body before help can arrive. This rapid onset is a significant factor in the high death toll.

- Illicit fentanyl is cheap and easy to produce, making it a preferred choice for dealers looking to increase profits. Its prevalence has transformed the drug supply into a deadly minefield.

To address this crisis, we must create a society where people feel safe seeking help for addiction. Judgment and criticism only push people further into isolation and shame, making recovery even more difficult. Here's how we can foster change:

- Equip communities with the knowledge to recognize addiction as a disease and understand the dangers of fentanyl.
- Advocate for expanded access to addiction treatment programs.
- Encourage open conversations about substance use and recovery. Create safe spaces where people can share their struggles without fear of judgment.
- Support legislation that prioritizes treatment over punishment, addresses the mental health crisis, and combats the illegal production and distribution of fentanyl.

Let's work together to end the stigma, support recovery, and stop the fentanyl crisis in its tracks. Logan's story, and the stories of countless others, can inspire the change we so desperately need. Together, we can make a difference.

The traumatic grief of losing a loved one, particularly a child, to fentanyl poisoning is an immensely challenging and multifaceted experience. For a parent, the loss is not just of the child but of the hopes, dreams, and shared moments they envisioned for the future. When fentanyl poisoning is the cause, it adds layers of complexity, including feelings of shock, guilt, anger, and a profound sense of injustice.

Fentanyl poisoning is often unexpected and rapid. The loss can feel surreal, leaving the grieving parent in a state of disbelief, struggling to reconcile the abrupt end with the life that existed just moments before. Society often attaches stigma to deaths related to substance use. Parents may feel judged or blamed, which can prevent them from openly grieving or seeking support. This isolation compounds the pain, making the grief feel even heavier. Parents often replay moments leading up to the loss, questioning their decisions and wondering if something could have been done to prevent it. The "what-ifs" become a haunting refrain, feeding feelings of guilt.

Anger may arise toward those who distributed the drug, the systems that failed to address the fentanyl crisis, or even toward the person lost for the choices they made. This anger can be hard to process, especially when intertwined with deep love and sorrow.

Remembering Logan may bring both joy and pain. Parents may worry about focusing too much on our children's struggles and not enough on the beautiful, meaningful parts of their life.

Traumatic grief is not something to "get over." Instead, it's about learning to carry it alongside the love, hope, and memories of Logan. This involves accepting that grief will ebb and flow and allowing oneself to feel joy without guilt when it arises. Many find solace in turning their pain into action, such as raising awareness about fentanyl poisoning, advocating for better resources for those struggling with addiction, or simply sharing their story to break the stigma surrounding substance use and loss.

Honoring Logan's memory through rituals, such as celebrating his birthday, sharing his favorite meals, or creating art in his memory, can provide moments of connection and comfort. Grief shared is grief lessened. Support groups for parents who have lost children to substance use, therapy, or even informal conversations with understanding friends can help process the grief and feel less alone. Grieving parents often hold themselves to impossible standards. It's important to acknowledge that they did the best they could with the knowledge and resources they had at the time. Forgiving oneself is an essential part of healing.

Logan's life was more than his struggles. Focusing on the joy he brought, the lessons he taught, and the love shared helps reframe his story in a way that emphasizes his humanity and legacy rather than solely the manner of his passing.

Learning to live with grief doesn't mean leaving it behind. Instead, it's about finding a way to coexist with it while allowing love and meaning to grow alongside it. Logan's memory becomes a guiding light, not only in moments of sorrow but also in moments of joy and purpose.

I will always carry the weight of his loss, but within it lies the opportunity to honor his life by helping others, cherishing the good times, and allowing his story to create change.

Starting a conversation with loved ones about the dangers of overdose and fentanyl poisoning can feel daunting, but it's essential in raising awareness, breaking stigma, and potentially saving lives. It requires empathy, honesty, and a nonjudgmental approach. Here's some suggestions on how to navigate this sensitive topic effectively:

- Choose the Right Setting: Find a quiet, comfortable environment where distractions are minimal. Privacy is important to encourage open and honest dialogue.

- Be Non-Judgmental: Approach the conversation with empathy, not accusations or blame. Let them know your intention is to support and protect, not criticize.

- Start With a Personal Connection: Share why this topic matters to you. For example: "I've been learning about how dangerous fentanyl can be, and I'm really scared because I care so much about you." Or "I want to talk about something important because I've seen how this issue has hurt others, and I'd never want to lose you."

- Provide Accurate Information: Explain that fentanyl is a synthetic opioid that is 50-100 times more potent than morphine, and even a tiny amount can be fatal. Mention how it's often mixed into other drugs (e.g., cocaine, pills, heroin) without the user knowing, which increases the risk of accidental overdose.

- Use Relatable Stories: Share real-life examples (like Logan's story if appropriate) to illustrate the devastating impact of fentanyl poisoning. Personal stories make the risks feel more immediate and real.

- For Teens or Young Adults: Highlight the unpredictability of illicit drugs, even ones they may think are "safe" or "recreational." Focus on their goals and dreams, emphasizing that fentanyl poisoning can tragically cut those short. Example: "I know you've been working so hard at school/work. Taking something laced with fentanyl, even unknowingly, could take all that away in an instant."

- For Friends or Adults Who May Be at Risk: Approach with care, expressing concern about their well-being. Example: "I've heard about how fentanyl is being mixed into things people don't expect. I worry because I care about you, and I wouldn't want something like that to happen to you."

- Educate About Prevention: Emphasize the importance of avoiding any pills or drugs not prescribed by a trusted doctor or pharmacy. If recreational drug use is involved, talk about using test strips to check for fentanyl and the importance of never using alone.

- Explain Naloxone (Narcan): Teach them about the life-saving benefits of naloxone, a medication that reverses opioid overdoses. Consider carrying naloxone and offer to show them how to use it. Example: "There's this nasal spray called Narcan that can save someone's life in an overdose. I keep it just in case, and I can show you how to use it."

- Expect Pushback: Some people may feel invincible, deny the risk, or get defensive. Stay calm and avoid arguing. Acknowledge their feelings: "I know this might feel like it doesn't apply to you, but fentanyl is showing up in places no one expects, and I just want you to be safe."

- Plant the Seed: Even if they don't seem receptive at first, your words may resonate later. You're opening the door for future conversations.

- Be a Trusted Ally: Let them know they can come to you without fear of judgment or punishment if they ever need help.

- Provide Resources: Share information about hotlines, treatment options, or harm reduction programs. Some examples:
  - National Helpline: 1-800-662-HELP (SAMHSA)
  - Websites like Shatterproof or Partnership to End Addiction

- End With Love: Reaffirm that you care. Close the conversation by reiterating how much they mean to you and that you're always there for them. Example: "I just want you to be safe and happy. I love you, and I'm always here if you want to talk."

- Check In Regularly: Continue the dialogue over time, reinforcing the message while showing ongoing care and support.
- Stay Educated: Keep learning about fentanyl and substance use, so you're prepared to answer questions or guide them toward help if needed.

It's not just me grieving as a father having lost a son, our entire family is grieving. Each of us carries the weight of Logan's absence in our own way, and together we share the sorrow of his loss.

My father, with his unshakable faith, is mostly quiet about his grief. Occasionally, he brings up Logan in conversations, offering small memories or reflections that show how deeply Logan remains in his heart. He relies on his faith as a source of strength, and while he doesn't speak about Logan often, the moments when he does are powerful and filled with love.

My nieces, Elizabeth and Callie, mourn the loss of their cousin in their own unique ways. They shared a bond with Logan that was built on years of family gatherings, shared laughter, and a mutual understanding of the complexities of life. His death left a void in their lives, but they have turned their grief into action, advocating for greater awareness and understanding of the struggles Logan faced.

It wasn't until shortly after four years had passed that I was able to bring the family together for a meeting to shed some light on Logan's death and to share how I was working through the pain. My niece Callie played a pivotal role in making this gathering happen, helping to create a safe space for us to have these difficult conversations. That meeting marked a turning point for our family, a moment of healing where we began to face our grief collectively and openly.

On the fourth anniversary of Logan's death, I participated in a national talk show in Dallas. Although that episode never aired, the experience was transformative for me. Speaking publicly about Logan and our family's loss gave me the strength to have an honest and heartfelt conversation with my loved ones. It was as though that moment on the talk show, even unseen by the world, gave me the courage to face the depth of my own pain and to invite others into my journey of healing.

I'm including some posts from Elizabeth and Callie's social media here, as their words capture the profound impact Logan's life and death have had on them. Their posts reveal a common thread, a commitment to stopping the stigma surrounding addiction and mental health. They understand, as I do, that stigma is a barrier to seeking help, healing, and preventing tragedies like Logan's.

Elizabeth's post reads: August 31st is National Overdose Awareness Day. As some of you know, addiction and overdose have touched my life in many ways. I've lost multiple friends and family members to this. I've walked with loved ones through addiction and come out the other side. I'm a medical provider to many patients who struggle with dependence and addiction, many of who were prescribed these substances at one point or another. For years, I wasn't really sure how to face this loss, verbalize it, or navigate it. Our cousin lived with us for years. We grew up together. He was our big brother. He taught me how to laugh at myself, how to dance, and how to cannonball into the pool while yelling Ace Ventura quotes. We saw each other through heartbreak, joy, loss, all the things. He found himself embattled with addiction in the years leading up to his death, and we lost him to an overdose due to Fentanyl poisoning in 2020. Getting that call is not something I'd wish on anyone. Our last words exchanged were not what I wanted them to be, and I wish every day that he was still here making me laugh. I wish he could've met my son Wyatt and taught him all about comic books and movies like he taught me. He would've been the best uncle. He was an amazing person. Addiction is blind, and it doesn't care who you are, how big of a heart you have, how much money you have, or how many people love you.

If you know someone struggling with addiction or someone struggling in the role of loving an addict, reach out. Reach out to me! Reach out to support groups! Reach out to friends! So many of us have lost someone or have experienced struggling with this ourselves. There should be no shame, just support. Community is everything, and no one needs to forge these things alone.

Logan's dad, Doug Ballinger Jr., has found healing in helping others through this and bringing awareness to this issue, and I'm so proud of him for that. I'd like to air out some awareness and help where I can too.

We're all in this together, and it's time to drop the stigma and get to talking about this epidemic! Don't forget to wear your purple tomorrow and start getting comfortable with talking about the uncomfortable. Love you, Logie-bear. Miss you every day.

Callie's post echoes this sentiment: Today is National Overdose Awareness Day. On March 19th, 2020, our family lost one of our brightest members to an overdose/fentanyl poisoning. I've often hesitated to talk about it because of the stigma surrounding addiction, and I didn't want people to see or judge Logan only for his struggles because he was so much more. My cousin was awesome, funny, artistic, brilliant, and caring. He lived with us while he was in high school and became like a big brother to my sister and me, a role he embraced perfectly. He was my hero! No one was cooler in my eyes. He comforted me when I was scared, picked me up when I'd scraped my knee or fell off my scooter; he taught me how to not let the bullies get you down, and even did the annoying brotherly things like popping my toes, which he knew I hated. He introduced me to music, the Shins, Radiohead, Gorillaz, and we bonded over art, books, and deep conversations about the meaning of life. His heart was big, and his laugh was even bigger to match.

Grieving someone lost to addiction is hard. Writing these memories makes me ache for those times again, summers spent watching MTV, swimming in the pool, riding 4-wheelers at the lake, hanging in our grandparents' living room, and all the Christmases and holidays. There are days when it feels like he's still here, but then the crashing reality hits that he isn't. Other days, it becomes all too real that he's gone, and my mind tries to block it out so I don't have to face it. I know I'm not alone in this. Too many of us are losing loved ones and friends to the opioid epidemic. I'm thankful to my Uncle Doug Ballinger Jr., Logan's dad, who has helped our family understand addiction and shown us that it's okay to grieve out loud. By speaking about it, we raise awareness, and with awareness, lives get saved.

I'm tired of the stigma, I know many of us who have been affected are - I want to talk about my cousin. I want to share his story, his full story, about the good times and the hard times. I want others to learn from it, and I want those struggling not to be scared to seek help because of shame or judgment. We're in an unprecedented time with this epidemic, and I think we can all agree: we'd rather walk with someone through their recovery than walk without them on this earth.

If you're struggling, know there are resources to help you and a community to support you that offers care, listening and help. You are not alone. You are loved, you are important, and we want you here with us.

These posts reflect not only their love for Logan but also their commitment to ensuring his death was not in vain. They, like me, want to create a world where people feel supported, not shamed, when they need help.

As a family, we continue to grieve, but we also continue to fight. We fight to honor Logan's memory, to bring light to the darkness of addiction, and to make sure that no other family has to endure the pain we have. Our shared loss has united us in a mission to create change, one conversation at a time.

Here I am, 4 ½ years later, a week before Christmas. It's the fifth Christmas without my son here with me. As he grew into adulthood and the miles between us stretched, we didn't always get to spend Christmas together in person, but we stayed connected through long phone calls. It's different now, painfully so, because I know he can't physically be here anymore. There's no chance of a call, no familiar voice to bridge the gap. Still, I push on.

Lately, I've been trying to piece together what happened on that fateful day in May 2020. I pulled out the death certificate, the one produced after the toxicology report came back. I noticed the cause of death was listed as intoxication with fentanyl and cocaine. That struck me as odd, heroin had always been his drug of choice. The report left me with more questions than answers.

Determined to understand, I turned to the notes I'd kept and reached out to the victim advocate in Sarasota, someone I had spoken with back in May 2020. I asked if it was possible to receive a copy of the toxicology report and any police reports associated with his death. A few days later, my request was fulfilled. What I received was more than I expected: the entire police report, the toxicology findings, and even pictures from the scene.

Processing the loss of a loved one, especially my own child, often feels like trying to solve a puzzle with missing pieces. Understanding what happened to Logan has become an essential part of my grieving process.

In the police report, there's a transcript of the 911 call made by his roommate. She had tried to wake him up so he could get ready for work but found him unresponsive. The details I have are based on what she told the police and what she said during the call. She mentioned to the 911 operator that his breathing was shallow. She also told the police that Logan had been drinking and smoking marijuana the night before and speculated that he must have taken something else.

The timeline in the report shows that emergency services arrived just four minutes after she placed the call. During those minutes, she struggled to move Logan from the bed to the floor, as the 911 operator instructed. At 235 pounds, it couldn't have been easy for her. Just as she was preparing to begin CPR under the operator's guidance, the paramedics arrived. Tragically, within moments, the lead responder pronounced Logan dead.

What makes this harder to process is the knowledge that his roommate was also battling addiction. They had been trying to stay clean together, yet something went terribly wrong. One question haunts me above all others: why didn't they administer Narcan? Logan had survived previous overdoses because of Narcan; once on his birthday in 2019, and twice more in November of the same year. It had saved him before. Why wasn't it used this time?

I also can't understand why his roommate told paramedics he had been clean for a year. That simply wasn't true, and she knew it. Her statement makes me question everything, what she told the police, what truly happened that night, and whether Logan could have been saved.

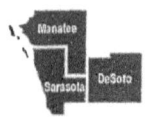

DISTRICT TWELVE MEDICAL EXAMINER

2001 Siesta Drive, Suite 302, Sarasota, FL 34239-2100 - Phone: (941) 361-6909 Fax: (941) 361-6914

TOXICOLOGY TESTING RESULTS

Decedent Information: Case #:   20-01218

Name:Rex Ballinger   Race: White   Gender: Male   Age: 32 Years

Specimen collected and submitted by: BROUSSARD, M.D., Wilson A

University of Florida Toxicology			4800 SW 35th Drive	
			Gainesville, FL 32608	
			Tel: (352) 265-0680 Fax: (352) 265-9904	
Test	Specimen	Substance	Result	Date
Comprehensive Drug Screen	Peripheral Blood	Benzoylecgonine	Positive Quantified_1211_ng/mL	8/13/2020
Comprehensive Drug Screen	Peripheral Blood	Cocaethylene	Positive (trace)_	8/13/2020
Comprehensive Drug Screen	Peripheral Blood	Cocaine	Positive (trace)_	8/13/2020
Comprehensive Drug Screen	Peripheral Blood	Gabapentin	Positive (trace)_	8/13/2020
Comprehensive Drug Screen	Urine	Benzoylecgonine	Positive_	8/13/2020
Comprehensive Drug Screen	Urine	Cannabinoids	Positive_	8/13/2020
Comprehensive Drug Screen	Urine	Cocaethylene	Positive_	8/13/2020
Comprehensive Drug Screen	Urine	Cocaine	Positive_	8/13/2020
Comprehensive Drug Screen	Urine	Gabapentin	Positive_	8/13/2020
Comprehensive Drug Screen	Urine	Levamisole	Positive_	8/13/2020
Comprehensive Drug Screen	Urine	Xylazine	Positive_	8/13/2020
Comments:	Tentative ID by GC-MS			
Drug Identification/Quantitation	Peripheral Blood	AcetylFentanyl	None Detected_	8/13/2020
Drug Identification/Quantitation	Peripheral Blood	Butyryl Fentanyl	None Detected_	8/13/2020
Drug Identification/Quantitation	Peripheral Blood	Fentanyl	Positive Quantified_8.9_ng/mL	8/13/2020
Drug Identification/Quantitation	Urine	AcetylFentanyl	None Detected_	8/13/2020
Drug Identification/Quantitation	Urine	Alfentanil	None Detected_	8/13/2020
Drug Identification/Quantitation	Urine	beta-Hydroxythiofentanyl	None Detected_	8/13/2020
Drug identification/Quantitation	Urine	Butyryl Fentanyl	None Detected_	8/13/2020
Drug Identification/Quantitation	Urine	Carfentanil	None Detected_	8/13/2020

As I reviewed the toxicology report, I found myself searching the internet for information about the substances detected in Logan's blood and urine. Traces of cocaine, gabapentin, and fentanyl were present, each raising its own set of questions. But there were two other substances that caught my attention: xylazine and levamisole. These unfamiliar names became my focus as I tried to piece together the puzzle of what caused his death.

Logan's drug of choice was heroin. He told me on several occasions that it was the only thing that could numb the pain he struggled with mentally. For someone suffering with SUDs, it often seems the driving force is to quiet the relentless noise in their minds. Not being someone suffering with SUD myself, I can only try to understand this through the lens of what I've learned: at first, the drugs seem to silence the pain, but over time, they take over every aspect of life. In the mind of an someone suffering with SUD, the drug becomes the noise, insistent and consuming, until it leaves no room for anything else.

I've come to realize that addiction is not just a battle against a substance but against an all-consuming force that distorts the very essence of a person. Life for someone with SUD is often reduced to a singular, desperate focus: finding the next fix. It's heartbreaking to think of Logan in this cycle, a young man who once had so many hopes and dreams, consumed by something he turned to for relief.

A wise woman once shared her own experience with me. She told me how, when her son overdosed, she prayed not only for him but also for the person who gave him the fatal pill. In her prayers, she felt a revelation: that someone suffering from heroin addiction may appear physically alive, was no longer fully himself. The addiction had taken over, becoming its own entity, living through him.

Her words have stayed with me, offering both clarity and anguish. It's a painful truth to confront, but it has also given me a way to frame Logan's struggles. His SUD didn't define who he was as a person, but it overshadowed the light that was truly him. As I learn more about the substances found in his system, I hope to better understand what led to his passing and, in some small way, find a measure of peace.

It's my belief that on that fateful night, Logan procured what he thought was heroin. Instead, what was injected into his right hand was likely a dangerous mixture of levamisole, xylazine, fentanyl and cocaine. The toxicology report showed no traces of heroin. This realization has been one of the hardest truths to process, as it means Logan may not have known the full danger of what he was taking.

Levamisole, a veterinary drug used to treat parasitic infections in animals, is a crystalline white powder. It's commonly used as a cutting agent in street drugs like cocaine to stretch supply and mimic certain effects. While cocaine is a stimulant that taps into the brain's reward system, creating feelings of euphoria, it's also insidiously dangerous. Prolonged use can lead to depression, psychosis, and severe heart problems, problems confirmed in Logan's autopsy report.

Then there's the xylazine. This non-opioid sedative, anesthetic, muscle relaxant, and pain reliever is intended strictly for veterinary use. It was never approved for humans due to its severe central nervous system depressant effects. Xylazine slows breathing, lowers heart rate, and induces profound sedation, which can lead to unconsciousness or death when combined with other drugs. On the streets, xylazine is increasingly mixed with fentanyl and other substances, creating a toxic cocktail that unsuspecting users believe to be heroin or another familiar drug.

Narcan, a life-saving drug that reverses opioid overdoses, has become a critical tool in combating the opioid crisis. However, xylazine presents a unique and devastating challenge: there is no reversal agent for its effects. Once xylazine begins to depress the central nervous system, there's little that can be done to revive someone, even if Narcan is administered. This makes xylazine-fentanyl combinations particularly lethal and compounds the already overwhelming challenges faced by first responders, those suffering with SUD, and their loved ones.

What makes xylazine even more terrifying is its availability. Despite requiring a veterinary license to purchase legally, it can be readily found on the internet, and accessible to virtually anyone. This unregulated access allows it to infiltrate street drugs with devastating frequency, further escalating the risk for unsuspecting users like Logan.

I believe Logan may have initially felt a familiar high after injecting what he thought was heroin. But as the xylazine took effect, it would have lulled him into a sleep from which he would never wake. I don't believe Logan intended to die that night. I believe he was overtaken by a combination of substances he didn't fully understand, a tragic testament to the unpredictability and danger of the drug supply on the streets.

As I struggle to put the pieces together, I often wonder if Logan knew he was dying, or if the drugs clouded his mind so thoroughly that he was unaware of death's approach. I truly hope it was the latter. The thought of him being conscious and unable to cry out for help is a heartbreaking image that lingers in my mind. It's a scenario no parent should ever have to imagine, let alone live with.

The growing prevalence of xylazine in street drugs is a public health crisis. It reflects the callous indifference of those who manufacture and distribute these substances, prioritizing profit over human lives. For Logan, and countless others like him, this toxic combination has stolen futures and shattered families. Understanding xylazine's role in the drug epidemic is a critical step in addressing the larger crisis and preventing more senseless tragedies.

We can, and should, focus efforts on addressing the supply side of the drug epidemic, tightening borders, arresting and prosecuting drug dealers, and stopping the flow of deadly substances onto our streets. These actions are necessary, but they are not enough. Until we address the root causes of substance use disorder, our society will continue to face a devastating cycle of senseless deaths and broken families.

Substance use disorder is not a moral failing or a lack of willpower, it's a complex and chronic illness that requires compassion, understanding, and evidence-based treatment. For many, addiction stems from unaddressed trauma, mental health challenges, or environments that leave individuals vulnerable to the pull of substances that promise temporary relief. Until we create a society that prioritizes mental wellness, builds accessible treatment options, and removes the barriers created by stigma, the battle against addiction will remain uphill.

By ending stigma, we can build a society where hope replaces shame, and where those in the grip of addiction have the support they need to reclaim their lives. Together, we can prevent more senseless losses and help families heal, one step at a time.

I've become involved with a group called the Hope Movement Coalition here in Arkansas. Our mission is twofold: to support families who have lost loved ones to overdose or fentanyl poisoning, and to raise awareness about this urgent societal crisis. We also celebrate those in recovery, offering encouragement and hope at every turn. This work is personal for me, as a father of an Angel, and I invite you to join us in being part of the solution.

It's going to take all of us, working together, to end this crisis. If you feel compelled to make a difference, I encourage you to visit the Hope Movement Coalition webpage. There, you'll find information about the work we're doing to turn our grief into purpose. Whether it's through spreading awareness, volunteering, or making a donation of any size, your support helps us in our mission to save lives and uplift families.

https://hopemovementcoalition.com

If you're not in Arkansas, I urge you to seek out and connect with a similar organization near you. This is not a crisis we can afford to ignore. Don't wait until it impacts your family, act now. Every effort, no matter how small it may seem, can make a difference.

I'd like to leave you with some cherished pictures of Logan throughout his life as well as messages from Uncle JD and Aunt Tammy. These reflections and images remind me of the love, joy, and light he brought to this world. His memory fuels my determination to create a better, safer future for others.

YOU ARE NOT ALONE

In Loving Memory of Logan

A Message From His Uncle JD

As I sit down to write this memorial for my beloved nephew Logan, I am overwhelmed with emotion. My heart feels broken, and I find it hard to articulate the depth of my grief. Sometimes, it seems easier to bury this pain deep inside, but I know that honoring Logan's memory requires me to confront these feelings head-on. Logan's journey through life was complex, and the paths he walked were not always easy. He faced the relentless pursuit of the monster of addiction, a struggle that I still grapple to understand. I often wonder why some endure and overcome while others, like Logan, seem trapped by their circumstances. It is a question that lingers, a reminder of our vulnerabilities and the randomness of life. The time spent at our Pecan Trees house was filled with heartfelt moments, love, celebration, victories, challenges, and times of defeat. Those memories are bittersweet; I wish I could have done more to help you, Logan. The feeling of helplessness weighs heavily on my heart, and I often find myself wishing I could have reached you in your darkest moments. But in remembering Logan, I also think of his incredible spirit. He had the best personality, a vibrant and loving heart that drew everyone in. His priorities always revolved around family and friends, and he cherished the connections he had with his cousins and stepcousins. Logan knew the importance of these bonds and often put them first in his life. He danced to his own beat, often with music blasting around him, a representation of his joy and individuality. Logan was a dreamer; he wanted to be a man of purpose with wholesome aspirations. Yet, the chaotic world around him served up too many options, shame, distractions, and defeats that made his journey harder. Today, we remember Logan not just for the struggles he faced but for the love he shared and the light he brought into our lives. His laughter, his passion for music, and his fierce loyalty to family will forever remain in our hearts. Though his journey has come to an end, we carry his spirit with us. Let us honor his memory by cherishing our connections, supporting one another, and understanding the importance of compassion in the face of struggles. Logan, you are loved beyond measure and will be deeply missed. Rest in peace, sweet nephew.

A Message from Aunt Tammy

I don't know how to process losing Logan. The pain is overwhelming. I'm heartbroken, angry, and consumed by guilt. I wish every day that I had done more. I knew he was struggling, but he kept me at arm's length. Our last conversation was a week before he passed. He called me on Mother's Day, crying and anguished over the loss of his mom and his two grandmothers. We talked for almost two hours about his feelings, his grief, his anger about the way his mother died, and his fear of letting us all down.

Toward the end of our conversation, he told me that his dad and he had arranged for him to go to rehab. I felt so relieved and hopeful, believing that this time it might truly work. He asked if he could come to stay with me after he got out, and I told him he would always have a home with me as long as I saw he was clean and committed to recovery. Before we ended the call, we said, "I love you." I told him how proud I was of his decision, and he said, "I don't want to die, Aunt Tammy." I promised him, "We have a plan to make sure that doesn't happen."

But then, less than a week later, Doug called to tell me that beautiful child was gone. I couldn't save him. I feel like I let Mom, Dad, and my sister down. I live with that every single day.

Doug, I am so proud of everything you're doing to honor Logan's memory. I loved that boy, no, that young man, so deeply.

Doug Ballinger

Letter from Teacher at Shirley High School

May 5, 2006

Logan,

I know that all the warm fuzzies were supposed to be written on the colorful paper, but when I started putting all of them together to write all of this....well, I just couldn't take it. So, I decided to type it all up for you. Here it goes...

I have tried my absolute best to make your senior year a good experience for you in SALC. I have done all I know how to do to get you through this program successfully. I hope you will take your fantastic thoughts for your future and turn them into a fabulous reality. We all have our cold prickleys that we MUST learn to overcome, but I want you to concentrate on all the warm fuzzies you have in your giant heart that you can share with everyone that loves you. You know I love you. I try to let you know that in some way everyday. There are more people that care about you than you will ever know. I am hoping that being in SALC has shown you a little about what it's like to have a stable, loving, supportive family by your side no matter what is going on in your life.

I try not to judge people before I get to know them. I'm glad I didn't go with my first impression of you, Logan. If I had, I don't know if we would have become as close as I feel like we are. I hope that you really and truly know that you can come to me and talk about anything at all. Sometimes I think you don't want me to know things, and that's fine, but I don't want you to dwell on things that you need to talk about. Does that make sense to you? I sure hope so. Ha-ha I know that this all probably sounds like rambling to you, but it is what I have been thinking about all afternoon. Mrs. Sandage got a phone call this afternoon from Mr. Moore telling her that you got into some trouble on the trip today. That is what got me thinking about all you are capable of doing if you only realized it. When she told me, all I could think was, "I'm gonna have to kill that boy before he will realize what he's doing." I just don't think you think things through before you do them sometimes. I know we all have our moments, but I don't understand why you are having so many of them lately. You are one of the most intelligent 18 year olds I have ever met in my life (and that's a long time). I want to see you accomplish all you dreams. OK, I'll stop with the lecture. I just wanted you to know some of what I think about you when you're not here. I told you the other day that when I'm not here with all of you I think about each and every one of you. You are just one that I wanted to know just exactly what goes through this crazy mind of mine. Well, maybe not EXACTLY!!! Ha-ha

I love ya, Logan. I know I don' have "the eyes" like Mrs. Smith does, but maybe I've got something to offer the world. Oh wait; I'll always have my math skills. Ya know, someday I'm gonna have to work on something else to impress. Ha-ha

Love,

Angie

Angie

P.S. I hope this wasn't all creepy or anything…getting something like this from a teacher, but I wanted to tell you what I think about you and I think you have the right to know.

Messages from Other Folks That Knew Logan

Logan, you were one of my best friends in high school and through college. We went to an ultra-music festival together. We used to ride around in your PT cruiser. You introduced me to Radiohead and Counterculture. You showed me the best movies and music. We shared hugs love and snuggles. I remember your mom and your da's. I remember visiting you at your grandparent's place in Naples. I still have the circle shelves you sold to me when you were working at the consignment store in Fort Lauderdale. You were such a huge part of my life and we lost touch because of distance and when I went to look for you to try to reconnect, I saw that you were gone and my heart broke! I just went to a movie at Paradigm in Fort Lauderdale and thought of you because the last time I was there was with you. I'll always remember our Randazzo days and your uniqueness. I love you forever and always.

Jessica – July 22, 2023 at 01:03 AM

Damn Logan, I can't believe this. My soul is so empty now. We last spoke on May 10th, Mother's Day, I never thought that would be the last time we spoke. You were the best friend I have ever had, despite the time and distance that separated us since Memphis. There's a hole now in my heart that can never be filled. You'll be missed bro but never forgotten.

PLUR grub Stephen – December 18, 2020, at 06:01 PM

Forever in our hearts. Logan had a huge heart, loved deeply, and a smile that would light up a room. Once in a while, someone comes into your life and it's like they've always been there. Logan, you were that someone. Gina and her "Bear" together forever. If only our love had been enough. I miss you.

Lori – May 30, 2020 at 05:27 AM

Doug and Dougie, Our sincere condolences to you and yours. Logan was a very special person. Many years ago (1992?) Logan was with Gina at our son's graduation in Wisconsin. Logan took an interest in his "Uncle Mark" and rarely left his side. Logan talked the entire way to the store and back again. Such an expressive child. He had long talks with Uncle Mark during Laurie's funeral and a few days after. So much potential! Our entire family will miss this man. Mark & Christine

Marc and Karen Marney and Bryan Rest in peace dear Logan. Sending our prayers to all.

My best friends, Gina, and Logan... gone from this earth, and finally peacefully together with no more pain. God bless you, Logan, you are loved.

Barbie – May 26, 2020 at 07:33 PM

Logan was such a good soul. We have so many memories that I'll always cherish. All of the laughs we shared at geckos, late-night hookah lounge trips, the good food, adopting Xena. He loved my son and was a light to my boyfriend and me in our darkest times. Missing you always Logan. Jewels & Tyler & Kai

Juliana - May 26, 2020, at 01:39 PM

Acknowledgments

This project would not have been possible without the support, guidance, and contributions of many individuals who have stood by me throughout this journey. Their kindness, wisdom, and encouragement have helped shape this work into what it is today.

To my family and friends, your love, patience, and shared memories have been invaluable. Your willingness to listen, to reflect, and to help me navigate the complexities of grief and advocacy has meant the world to me.

Logan was deeply loved by his mother, Gina, whose dedication and support never wavered, no matter the challenges. Her sister, Aunt Tammy, along with her children, Ashley Paull, Eric Kraus, and Jared Kraus held a special place in Logan's life, offering him love, laughter, and a sense of family that meant so much to him. His uncles, Kevin Hagberg, and Justin Hagberg, also played an important role in his journey, providing guidance and encouragement along the way. Their love and support for Logan were immeasurable, and their impact on his life will never be forgotten.

Logan was not alone in his struggle, and tragically, our family has felt the devastating impact of the opioid crisis more than once. He lost two beloved cousins, Justin Ballinger and Chase Lipsey, to this epidemic. Their lives were cut far too short, leaving behind memories cherished by those who loved them. May you both rest in peace. You are loved, you are missed, and you will never be forgotten.

To those who have dedicated their lives to fighting the stigma surrounding addiction and mental health, your work is a beacon of hope. Whether you are a parent who has lost a child, an educator offering second chances, a recovery advocate, or simply someone willing to have hard conversations, you are making a difference.

A special thanks to Staci James and all the warriors of the Hope Movement Coalition, as well as the incredible group of people who stand with me in this battle. Your unwavering love, support, and dedication have not only fueled my passion but have truly saved my life. Together, we fight to bring hope, awareness, and change, honoring those we've lost and protecting those still struggling. I am forever grateful to each and every one of you.

And to Logan, this is for you.

Your story matters,

Your life mattered,

And I will continue to be your voice.

Gran and her grandchildren, Callie, Logan, and Elizabeth

Logan, Callie, and Elizabeth in Gran and Granddaddy's backyard

Doug Ballinger

Logan and his dog

Logan and his mom, Gina

Doug Ballinger

Celebrating Cindy's Birthday

Logan And His Dad

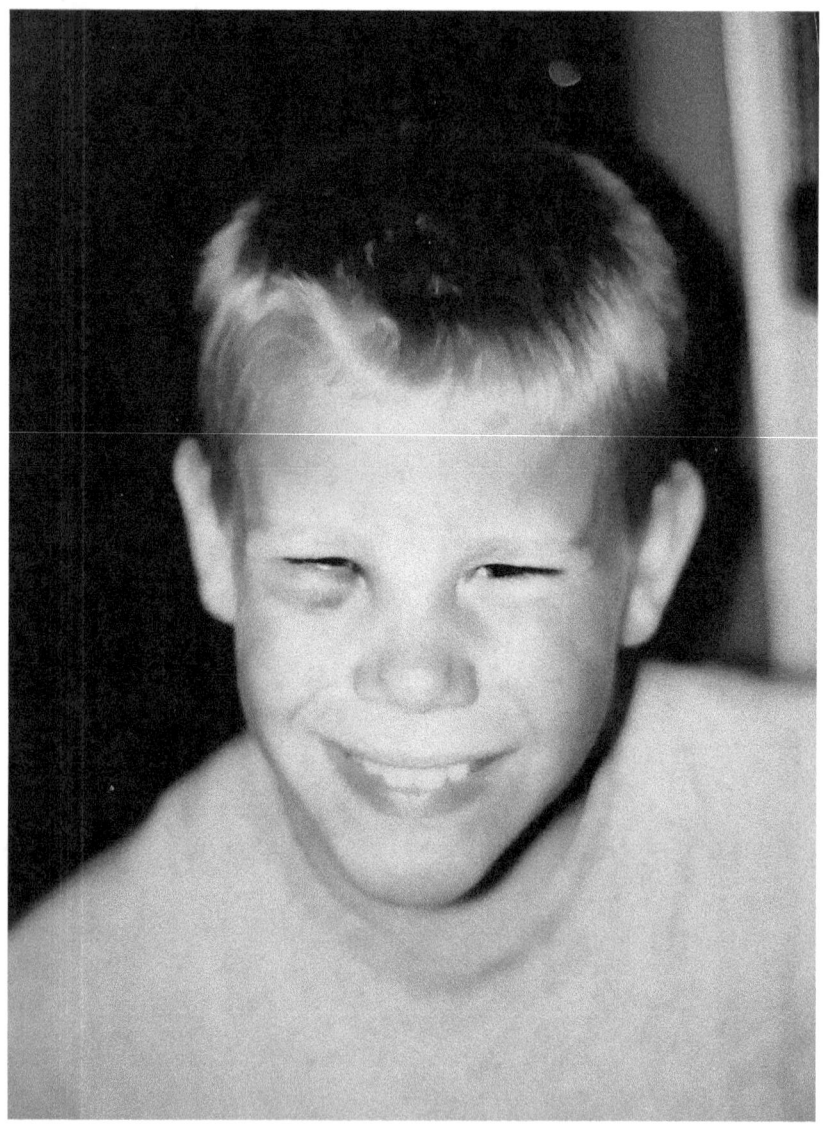

Boys will be boys

Logan reflecting on life

Logan was the DJ at a party in Miami

Logan

Doug Ballinger

Logan and Dad on a Deep-Sea Fishing Excursion

Logan looking "cool" as always

Logan and his mom

Logan and his cousins, Jared, Ashley and Erik

Logan Smiles

Logan and I

Logan and Grandaddy

Logan with Gran and Grandaddy

Logan and Daniel

logan and uncle JD

\Logan and Dad

Logan with his cousins Elizabeth and Callie

This is the last picture Logan and I took together. It was in Sarasota in January of 2020

Thanks to everyone who contributed to this project.
Your support helps to tell Logan's Story.

Suzanne Clark

Alaina Roberts

Wendy & John Lokay

Christopher Dickie

Bridget Lipsey

Kimmy & JD Ballinger

Lauren Wolfe

Laura Reeves

Callie & Ken Billman

Mary Carmack

Missy Treece

Cindy Carmack

Rebecca Mahmood

Celeste Pryor

Mary Ann Parker

Laura & Steve Lee

Ashlyn & Hunter Everett

Randy Sellers

Kimberly Ross

Dee Brigman

David Carmack

Cynthia Wolfe

Patricia Stringer

Cammie Rice

Kelly Lipsey

Winnie & Doug Ballinger, Sr.

Kristen Taylor

Shane Mason

Whitney Everett

Debra Johnson

Lori Carter

Elizabeth & Peyton Sweeney

Vanessa Scroggins

Molly Barbosa

David Costello

Susan McCabe

Cheryl Campbell

Cheryl McCabe

Campbell Duffy

Shane Mason

Carolyn Keeling

Lori Chinske

Deb Nunez

www.ingramcontent.com/pod-product-compliance
Lightning Source LLC
Chambersburg PA
CBHW071714120626
46550CB00001B/233